# The ABCs of Choosing a Good Husband

# The ABCs of Choosing a Good Husband

Stephen Wood

Family Life Center Publications

ISBN: 0-9658582-4-3
Library of Congress Control Number: 2001-131200
Book production and design: Family Life Center Publications
Cover design: Catherine Wood
Manufactured in the United States of America

## Acknowledgments

I would like to thank my wife, Karen, and my daughter,
Stephanie, for their advice, encouragement, and proofreading.
I also thank my daughter, Catherine, for the creation of the cover
design. I express special gratitude to Mike Phillips, Rick
Sarkisian, Philip Cutajar, and Paul Thigpen for their proofreading, editing, and scores of helpful suggestions. I thank two
members of my staff, Lucy Allen and Marie Roche, for their
assistance in obtaining quotations, statistics, and resources used
in this book.

Family Life Center Publications
22226 Westchester Blvd.
Port Charlotte, FL 33952
www.familylifecenter.net

# Dedication

Dedicated to the six precious girls God has sent into my life:
Stephanie, Catherine, Anne, Sarah, Mary and Susan. If God calls
you to marriage, my prayer is that you may experience all the
joy in wedlock that I have experienced with your mother.

# Contents

# A Word of Introduction

Who wants to be bound to a lifetime of unhappiness? Today, women are increasingly pessimistic about finding satisfying, lifelong love in marriage. The high rate of divorce has eroded expectations for the possibility of permanent commitment. Increasingly, women are either postponing marriage or are hesitant about ever entering into it.

Don't lose heart. It's fully possible in today's world to find and marry a man who will love you and be faithful to you "till death do you part." Amidst the wasteland of shattered marriages, you *can* find happiness in lasting marital love.

Things work best when you use them as originally intended. I keep warning my younger children that cabinet hinges will bend if used as swings, arms of chairs will crack if used as stools, and beds will break if used as trampolines.

Similarly, over the course of the twentieth century we've ignored God's original intent, His design, for lasting love. This neglect has created a desert of broken marriages, as well as a mountain of incredible heartache. Happiness in marriage begins long before you say, "I do." By rediscovering and practicing the divine design for courtship *before* marriage, you'll help ensure lasting love and fulfillment *in* marriage.

The sources I used to write this little book were many: Scripture, Church teachings about marriage, timeless wisdom from past generations, contemporary research on marriage and family life, my personal experiences from twenty-two years of marriage, and my experience helping other married people in counseling—along with a healthy dose of common sense.

I found the idea for the *ABCs of Choosing a Good Husband* in a three-thousand-year-old portion of the Old Testament. In Proverbs chapter 31, a queen mother teaches her son the characteristics to look for in a wife. Verses 10 through 31 present an acrostic poem in Hebrew; that is, each verse begins with a letter of the Hebrew alphabet in alphabetical order. This literary device was used to project an "A-to-Z" picture of the ideal wife for the guidance of the royal prince.

Since I have the rare blessing of being the father of six daughters, I felt a strong need to transform the ABCs of finding the ideal wife into a corresponding guide for choosing a good husband. To make a wise choice in a husband, you need to know a fair amount about both men and marriage. My hope is that my daughters and many other women will find this book useful, and that they'll take wise steps towards building a successful, deeply fulfilling, and happy marriage.

You'll find the ABCs direct and challenging, but they can serve as a template for your selection of a husband. I'm confident that by following *all* of the ABCs, you can lessen the likelihood of divorce by at least seventy-five percent. Remember this, however: Your marriage will benefit only to the degree that you put into practice what you read.

## CHAPTER ONE

# A

# Attract a Man Who Will Love You as a Person

John Blanchard stood up from his seat and straightened his neatly pressed army uniform as he studied the crowd of people making their way through Grand Central Station in New York. He eagerly looked for the girl whose heart he knew, but whose face he didn't—the girl with the rose.

His interest in her had begun two years before in a Florida library. Taking a book off the shelf, he found himself intrigued, not with the words of the book, but with the notes penciled in the margins.

The soft handwriting reflected a thoughtful soul and an insightful mind. In the front of the book, he discovered the previous owner's name: Miss Holly Maynell. In time and with some effort he located her address. She now lived in New York City.

He wrote her a letter introducing himself and inviting her to correspond. The next week he was shipped overseas for duty in World War II.

During the next two years they grew to know each other through overseas mail. Each letter was a seed falling on a fertile heart. A romance was budding. Blanchard requested a photograph, but she refused. She felt that, if he really cared, it wouldn't matter what she looked like.

When the day finally came for him to return from Europe, they scheduled their first meeting at 7:00 P.M. at the train station. "You'll recognize me," she wrote, "by the red rose I'll be wearing on my lapel." So at 7:00 P.M. sharp he was in the station looking for the girl whose heart he loved, but whose face he'd never seen.

In Mr. Blanchard's words, this is what happened next:

> A gorgeous young woman was coming toward me, her figure long and slim. Her blond hair lay back in curls from her delicate ears; her eyes were as blue as flowers. Her lips and chin had a gentle firmness, and in her pale green suit she was like springtime come alive.
>
> I started toward her, entirely forgetting to notice that she was not wearing a rose. As I moved, a small smile curved her lips. "Going my way, soldier?" she murmured. Almost uncontrollably I made one step closer to her—and then I saw Holly Maynell.
>
> She was standing almost directly behind the girl. A woman well past forty, she had graying hair tucked under a worn hat. She was more than plump, with her thick-ankled feet thrust into low-heeled shoes. The girl in the green suit was walking quickly away. I felt as though I was split in two, so keen was my desire to follow her, and yet so deep was my longing for the woman whose spirit had truly been my companion overseas.
>
> And there she stood. Her pale, plump face was gentle and sensible, her gray eyes had a warm and

12

kindly twinkle. I did not hesitate. My fingers gripped the small, worn copy of the book that was to identify me to her.

This would not be love, but it would be something precious, something perhaps better than love, a friendship for which I had been and must ever be grateful. I squared my shoulders, saluted, and held out the book to the woman, even though while I spoke I felt choked by the bitterness of my disappointment. "I'm Lieutenant John Blanchard, and you must be Miss Maynell. I am so glad we could meet; may I take you to dinner?"

The woman's face broadened into a tolerant smile. "I don't know what this is about, son," she answered, "but the young lady in the green suit who just went by, she begged me to wear this rose on my coat. And she said that if you were to ask me out to dinner, I should tell you that she is waiting for you in the big restaurant across the street. She said it was some kind of test!"[1]

## The right way to attract a man

Miss Maynell was a wise woman. Your goal, like hers, is to get acquainted with a man in such a way that he'll be attracted to you as a person and not as an object.

Multitudes of men are seeking an exciting weekend date, a poster girl, a six-month playmate, or a trophy wife. Such playboys are selfish, pleasure-seeking, and immature—incapable of lasting love. On the other hand, many good men would be eager to love you for who you really are. The question is, how can you attract this second kind of man while avoiding the first kind?

A woman wishing to attract a man who will love her as a person must dress and act with modesty. God went way overboard for Adam when He created Eve. He designed a woman's body to radiate more beauty than any of His works. He fully intends for a woman's body to be physically appealing to a man.

Yet God also designed a woman's body as a sacred mystery to be unveiled only to her husband. To *profane* means to make common what God has set apart as sacred. A lack of modesty in a very real way profanes the sacredness of your beauty.

You may not be aware of this, but every woman sends out signals to men. Most men can detect and read your signals in a matter of seconds. The first pulses you emit are your dress and your body language (that is, your deportment).

It's incredibly easy for a woman to attract attention from men. Just wear skin-tight, thigh-length, revealing clothing. You'll get lots of male attention. Guaranteed. But will it be the kind of attention you want?

## Modesty protects you from immature men

Fishermen insist that the fish you catch is determined by the bait you use. Do you want to fend off the playboys incapable of real love? Then don't dress like a playgirl. Do you want to be the type of woman who's attractive to a good man who'll want to bring you home to meet his folks? Then dress like one. You'll largely determine how a man will relate to you through your modesty, or lack thereof.

Modesty protects you from men capable of only superficial love. Remember, your physical appearance will change over the next three or four decades. How will you know whether your husband will still love you then? Will you be abandoned for an attractive young co-worker, or will you enjoy the years with a man who has lifelong allegiance to you? Learn from Miss Maynell to attract the type of man who will faithfully love you as a person.

## CHAPTER TWO

# B

# Before You Say, "I Do" . . . Beware of the "Trigger Effect"

You were thrilled to meet, fall in love with, and marry Mr. Right. You didn't spend much time learning about his parents and family experiences. Why bother? You found him to be a caring and kind gentleman during your dating.

Then you were shocked a few months after the honeymoon, or after the birth of your first child, when he seemed to change dramatically—for the worse. Now he doesn't even seem to be the man you married. What happened?

I call it the "trigger effect." Many people have unresolved childhood conflicts lying dormant inside them. Living together before marriage often allows these conflicts to remain hidden, but the pivotal events of marriage or the birth of a child have the potential to trigger their reappearance unexpectedly. The result can be monumental personal and marital difficulties such as uncontrollable anger, irritability, alcoholism, inability to demonstrate affection, eating disorders, or an irrepressible urge to control and dominate.

## The surprising impact of past family life

Obviously, you want to minimize the possibility that the trigger effect could explode in your marriage. To save yourself a life of misery, then, you must pay attention to this critical truth about family life: *We all bring our past family life into our marriages.* The family backgrounds of both spouses have a continuing impact on their married life, for better or for worse. So you need to investigate carefully the family background of any potential spouse if you don't want to encounter unpleasant surprises when it's too late.

If you or your potential husband come from a family with a history of alcoholism or drug addiction; sexual, physical, or verbal abuse; serious psychological problems; or divorce—then you must be aware that your marriage *will* have additional strains.

You might ask, "How could a divorce in my fiancé's family background possibly affect our future relationship, since we're both Christians committed to lifelong marriage?" Everyone, even a committed Christian, is deeply affected by his family history. A child's bad family experiences can exert a strong negative influence on his marriage as an adult.

## Fatherlessness and immature manhood

Take the example of a boy who grew up in a broken home where Mom and Dad divorced while he was in grade school. A young boy is naturally drawn into a close attachment to his mother. Being a "mama's boy" under seven years of age is fine and healthy. And yet for a boy to mature fully in his masculinity, he needs to "detach" from Mom and form a closer attachment with his father throughout older boyhood and adolescence.

A boy matures into manhood through this close identification with his father. Once a young man has fully matured in this way, he's ready for a close reattachment to a woman—his wife. But it's extremely difficult for a boy to mature in his masculinity without the presence of a father. The need for a good father to prepare a young man for marriage can be easily obscured *before* marriage, but the absence of mature masculinity becomes painfully obvious *within* marriage.

What should you do if a man you're interested in comes from a divorced, dysfunctional, or abusive family background? In the past, I would have just pointed out the potential for additional marital problems. Today, I would issue a strong caution *and* recommend skilled, professional counseling—*before* accepting a proposal.

## Choose a counselor carefully

A word of warning about counselors is in order. There are probably more ineffective, incompetent, or dysfunctional marital therapists and psychologists than there are good ones. You're better off without any counseling at all than with bad counseling. Yet the value of a good counselor is priceless to those who require assistance.[2]

Many people—through heroic efforts, good counsel, and dependence upon God's grace—have learned the skills to cope with their background conflicts. Others think they have magically escaped being scarred by family dysfunction only to find the sudden and unexpected reappearance of negative behaviors in the first few years of marriage. *Before* you get engaged, find out if anything in the family background has the potential to launch the "trigger effect." If so, then obtain the finest counseling available *before* taking any further steps toward marriage.

## CHAPTER THREE

# C

# Challenges Attract the Best Men

Men have always been internally wired to love a *real* challenge. Some contemporary "experts" think that modern men have lost this basic male drive. They're crazy.

Have you ever wondered why one particular branch of the U.S. military never seems to have a problem meeting its recruiting quotas? The Marines demand the most from their recruits, and they never fail to attract highly committed young men. You, too, can attract a highly committed husband by keeping your standards high.

## The "disposable date"

Some women fear that if they don't throw themselves at men, they'll never find a husband. But the opposite is true. Sure, many men like an exciting date who "gives in" easily. But such a woman is quickly tossed aside while the man she thought was in love with her seeks his next cheap thrill.

Besides suffering the heartache of becoming the "disposable date," the woman who lowers her standards is the woman least likely to find a faithful husband. Do you want to be a playboy's toy for an evening or the kind of woman a good man is happy to love the rest of his life?

## Allow a man to initiate

Don't fawn over a man you're attracted to. Maintain a warm, friendly, and courteous reserve. Allow him to take the lead. It's wise for the man to initiate the courting. This time-tested approach recognizes some of the subtle yet significant differences between men and women. Don't tinker with a pattern proven by centuries of experience. Besides, do you really want to marry a man who can't initiate your courtship himself?

## Keep your standards high

Be courageous enough to raise your moral standards and marital expectations, and the really good men will be attracted to the challenge of courting you. Women have the ability either to bring out the best in men or to help them persist in immaturity. The more effort your future husband puts into meeting the challenge of your standards and expectations, the more he'll appreciate you as a person and as a wife.

You might be asking yourself, "How will I ever find a husband if I do that? There aren't a thousand men in the whole country who would meet my highest standards for a husband." There may not be a thousand, or even a hundred, men who will meet your standards. That's okay. The Marines can win battles with "a few good men." All you need for a husband is *one* good man. Keep the challenge high in your courtship, and you'll find the man with whom you want to spend a lifetime.

## CHAPTER FOUR

# D

# Dating or Courtship?

Dating creates a series of temporary, emotionally based, romantic relationships. "Going steady" intensifies dating relationships by creating "mini-engagements," as well as the subsequent heartbreaks caused by "mini-divorces." Is dating's pattern of bonding and breaking up better preparation for lifelong marriage, or for today's familiar cycle of marriage, divorce, and remarriage?

## Dating only as old as the automobile

Dating is mainly a twentieth-century phenomenon. You might be surprised to learn that the history of dating is no older than the automobile.

One book on the demise of courtship is aptly titled *From Front Porch to Back Seat*.[3] The car took young couples and courtship away from their families. While providing what seemed to be exciting new freedoms, it had disastrous consequences for marriage.

## Dating leaves out the family

Dating usually involves very little time with families and much more time alone as a couple or with peers. Only in "enlightened" societies were people crazy enough to think this was a good preparation for enduring marriage. For the rest of the history of the world, and in all cultures, the family circle was recognized as the best environment to get to know a potential marriage partner.

## Double-dating (frequently double trouble)

Time away alone together, or even with peers, is prime time for premarital sex. The more time alone together, the higher the probability of premarital relations. Some chastity "experts" imagined that double-dating was the perfect deterrent to immorality in dating. But the reality is that double-dating with peers is usually "double trouble."

The younger a person begins dating, the higher the probability that she'll engage in premarital sex. What's the problem with that? Plenty. In the next chapter you'll see how premarital sex is absolutely guaranteed to weaken your future marriage.

## Courtship within the family circle

Unlike dating, courtship takes place in the context of family life. It's a relationship between a young man and a young woman who are seeking a partner for marriage. The separation from family during dating removes all the protective guidance a mother and father can offer their daughter. In contrast, all the strength of the family is placed at your disposal during courtship.

Exactly how do you court in the twenty-first century? The skills needed for the art of courtship have been lost, and we all need to rediscover them. For starters, you can rethink how you use a car.

I know this sounds radical, but I suggest that a car be used only for chaperoned social activities and to visit each other's homes, if they are nearby. You, and the man courting you, should interact with your families at mealtimes and join in family activities, recreation, and outings as much as possible. Don't use a car for private times together. Your family should provide some semi-private "space," such as the family room or the front porch, for the two of you to talk together.

## Courtship and communication

Verbal communication is a primary way that husbands *should* express love for their wives. Yet the lack of genuine communication by men in marriage is deeply troubling to millions of wives. It is, in fact, a prime reason why women decide to give up on their marriages and divorce their husbands.

You'll never know whether your prospective spouse can communicate if your communication consists mainly in steaming up the back of a car. Get your relationship out of the back seat and return it to the front porch, where real love can be communicated.

## College courtship

What if your family's home is far away? It's hardly unusual today for a young woman to live at some distance from her family. But few have ever considered the impact of the loss of immediate family support for young women trying to find a marriage partner. If college or some other necessity takes you away from your family, you'd be wise to seek out a "mentoring couple" who can become actively involved in your courtship process away from home.

Organizations such as Marriage Savers are having fantastic success using mentoring couples in churches. These mentors assist couples during engagement and in the early years of marriage.[4] Why not extend this extremely successful strategy to courtship as well? Your mentoring couple might be a faculty couple or a couple you meet in a local parish.

Should you find courtship mentors, keep in mind that they should never totally supplant your own parents in this role. I suggest that you use your vacations to court within your immediate family circle. You'd also be wise to consult your parents when choosing a mentoring couple; you'll want the best example of a loving, Christian family for this important role.

If your family isn't nearby, or a committed mentoring couple isn't available, then at least you can spend your courting time together in chaperoned group social activities. For instance, if you're away at college, a few courting couples could go out to dinner with a young faculty couple for an enjoyable evening.

## Preserving physical intimacy for marriage

I can just hear it now. "Chaperones! You've got to be kidding. Aren't chaperones for little kids' dances and for people who lived in the Dark Ages?"

No, chaperones have been appreciated by wise people in every age—people who realize that it's all too easy for a Christian couple to become physically intimate before marriage, thereby weakening their relationship. Using a chaperone is one of the time-tested methods of preserving physical intimacy for marriage. It's valued by those who treasure lasting love.

Chaperones and the family courting circle were abandoned in the early twentieth century for the thrill of the automobile and the "independence" provided by the dating revolution. Is it a wonder that throughout the last century the incidence of premarital sexuality skyrocketed, leaving millions of broken hearts, shattered families, and fatherless children? Isn't it past time that we return to the practices that directly involve families and chaperones in preserving lasting love?

## Dads elevate the courting relationship

Even if you're away at college, a young man should ask for your father's permission before you start any serious courting. It may sound overly strict or passé, but this time-honored practice will surely experience a revival as courtship spreads across campuses. Already, at least one Christian college in America, with considerable foresight, requires students who intend to date seriously "to notify the families and follow parental rules on courtship."[5]

Having a young man call your father for permission will elevate your courting relationship to an entirely different and higher plane. You'll be appreciated more and treated with greater respect. A genuinely respectful young man won't hesitate to accept your father's advice and authority—even though he might be a little nervous calling your dad.

## Dads help to filter out phonies

Some guys, without having the slightest thought of a long-term commitment, will say sweet things in order to get a girl to respond to their selfish desires for pleasure. How do you filter out these phony Romeos?

Having a guy call your dad is an easy, quick, and painless way to separate the wheat from the chaff among your suitors. It takes a little guts for a young man to call your father. But a guy who is really interested in *you* will do it.

## Let your dad dump the duds

Having a young man call your father carries a special bonus. Your dad can do the dirty work that many young women find difficult to do. I'm talking about the difficulty women have in saying no to a man they're not interested in. If you find it difficult to say no, then let your dad do it for you.

## When are you and a particular man ready to court?

Dating is done just for the fun of it, without marriage in mind. It's only a game between the sexes. But courtship is much more.

The purpose of courtship is to discover whether it's really God's will for a couple to enter marriage. For that reason, courtship presupposes that both the man and woman are spiritually, emotionally, and financially ready for marriage. A young man is ready to begin courting you when he has the maturity to enter marriage and is skilled enough in his vocation to begin supporting a family.

### Avoiding *Peter Pan*

Courtship isn't for immature men void of self-discipline, who lack the ability to make and keep commitments, who sleep until noon, who lack employment and training, who hang out all the time at the mall blowing their money on the latest CDs. So how can you avoid marrying a *Peter Pan* type—one who never wants to grow up?

The easiest way to remain free from entanglement to an immature man is never to begin a relationship with one! Save your heart for a man who's ready for marriage, and then begin courtship to determine whether the two of you are really meant to be married.

Courtship will gain popular appeal in our culture as positive results are demonstrated in the lives of twenty-first century "courtship pioneers." We should start seeing the verifiable beneficial results of courtship, such as fewer divorces and higher marital satisfaction, within a decade or two. In the meantime, if you want your future marriage to last a lifetime, and you don't want to become another "dating game" statistic, then be among those who have chosen the courtship path—the path leading to lifelong marriages.

## CHAPTER FIVE

# E

# Extinguishing *Real* Love—Before Your Marriage Begins

Currently, the average marriage in the United States that ends in divorce lasts about seven years. About twenty percent of divorcing couples end their marriage before their third anniversary. The majority of filings for these divorces are made by women. In the face of such gloomy statistics, no wonder young women are becoming increasingly pessimistic about marriage. But is the problem really with marriage, or with what goes on before marriage?

## "Trial marriages" lead to broken relationships

Anyone can understand why a young couple in our divorce-prone society would want to take precautionary steps to make sure they're really suited for each other. A common way couples do this is by living together in a "trial marriage," to see if they're really compatible. Research shows that the majority of high schoolers and college students think that living together improves the chances for a successful marriage. In fact, more than half the couples getting married today have lived together first, up from ten percent in 1965.

On the surface this seems to make sense. Everyone knows that you take a car out for a test drive before purchasing it. Certainly you want to try on a dress before buying it—even if it's on sale.

In a similar vein, it seems natural to imagine that a "trial" marriage will improve your chances for marital success. Yet in reality, the opposite is likely to occur. Striking statistical evidence shows that if you have sex before marriage you'll *increase* the odds of divorce by at least forty-five percent![6]

Research by the Rutgers University Marriage Project found that cohabiting couples are more prone to develop negative individualistic attitudes that undermine genuine love. The Marriage Project also found that cohabiting couples are less happy in marriage and less sexually faithful to their partners than couples who did not live together before marriage. Only one in six cohabiting couples enjoys a relationship that lasts longer than three years.[7]

## Unexpected problems from cohabitation

Cohabitation destroys love and marriage for at least four reasons.[8] First, living together kills the motivation for men even to begin a marriage.

Researchers have found that women typically expect a few months of living together to be adequate for getting to know a man well enough to form a permanent relationship. On the other hand, the young men reported that they would be happy to cohabit indefinitely.[9] Yet cohabitation encourages persistent immaturity in men. It enables men to enjoy the physical pleasures of a relationship without meeting the demands of commitment and self-sacrificing love required in a marriage.

Second, since cohabiting relationships are usually brief, these men and women inevitably go through repeated heart-wrenching breakups. Author Barbara Dafoe Whitehead states that "each successive relationship starts out at a lower level of trust and commitment than the one before."[10] These downwardly spiraling cycles cannot help but weaken trust and commitment, two of the ingredients necessary for a successful marriage.

Third, cohabitation creates selfishness—the enemy of true love. The marital embrace is designed by God to be a total, self-giving experience. So before you enter the marital embrace, you need to take the vital step of pledging yourself in the marriage vows.

Exchanging vows is not just a nice touch at a wedding ceremony. These vows mysteriously and profoundly cement your souls together in the deepest part of your being. The self-giving and mutual joining, expressed through your vows, need to precede the self-giving of the marital embrace. When the pleasure of sexual relations is sought apart from the vows of lifelong love and fidelity, then this embrace is degraded into an act of selfishness.

Fourth, cohabitation increases the probability of divorce because of its effect on marital communication. As we noted before, a primary way you'll receive love from your future husband is through verbal communication. Women have a deep and continuing need to receive verbal expressions of love from their husbands. Yet premarital relations increase the chances that your future husband will be permanently tongue-tied. A study by the National Council on Family Relations found that newlywed wives who had engaged in premarital relations complained of poor communication after the wedding.[11]

## The need for premarital communication

Why is this true? For starters, you must realize that there's a vast difference between the communication styles of men and women. Simply put, men talk far less than women about feelings.

During the critically important months before marriage, your fiancé needs to learn how to overcome his natural reluctance to express his love to you in verbal ways. Sure, he'll feel physical urges. But if these are restrained through mutual self-control, his verbal skills will have a chance to develop.

On the other hand, if you engage in physical relations before marriage, the overwhelming intensity of physical communication will eclipse the verbal. Your fiancé won't be able to imagine what "better" communication could possibly take place. Thus at the very stage in your developing relationship when emotional bonding through verbal communication should be flourishing, your fiancé will end up with fast-frozen communications skills.

After about seven years of waiting for the big thaw (which never takes place), millions of wives lose all hope of ever receiving emotional support from their husbands. Many of them file for divorce. The divorcing wife says, "You don't love me," while the baffled husband is without a clue as to what happened.

Why extinguish real love in your marriage before it begins? Avoid cohabitation. If you're currently in a cohabiting relationship, then put down this book and make a change immediately. I mean right now! Take whatever steps are necessary to end cohabitation. Recovering a chaste courtship will dramatically improve your chances for a successful marriage.

Before God gave His commandments, He wasn't up in heaven wondering, "How can I mess up people's lives and rob them of happiness and pleasure?" No, the Bible says that God gave us His commandments for our good (Deuteronomy 10:13). God's commandment to reserve sexual intimacy for marriage is His gracious safeguard for true love. Keep to His path and find lasting happiness in marriage.

## CHAPTER SIX

# F

# Family Finances

There's no escaping the reality: money matters in marriage. The number-one topic in marital fights is money. Husbands and wives commonly develop bitterness toward each other over family finances. Money squabbles easily escalate into domestic wars that end in divorce.

## Preventing the financial tug-of-war

To prevent a financial tug-of-war from ruining your future marriage, make use of a proven strategy: turn over the ownership of all your assets to God. That's right. Give God one hundred percent of your money market funds, stocks and mutual funds, checking account balances, IRAs, real estate, the title to your car . . . all of it.

Does this mean that you and your future husband will have to live in abject poverty? No, God doesn't expect you to be penniless. But He does want you to acknowledge formally that all you have comes from His gracious hand.

You reinforce this commitment by regularly tithing ten percent of all your financial increase. Tithing (giving ten percent) is the divine remedy for preventing the human heart from getting too greedy. Tithing also minimizes the *his-vs.-hers* financial tug-of-war, since both of you regularly acknowledge God to be the owner of all your assets.

## Money affects the heart and the heart affects marriage

Money deeply affects the human heart. St. Paul warned, "Those who desire to be rich fall into temptation, into a snare, into many senseless and hurtful desires that plunge men into ruin and destruction. For the love of money is the root of all evils; it is through this craving that some have wandered away from the faith and pierced their hearts with many pangs" (1 Timothy 6:9-10).

Every couple needs to maintain constant vigilance against an inordinate love of money. If you allow money to displace the love of God in your hearts, then marital love evaporates as well.

Make sure the man you marry honors God with his money by tithing. You want to marry a generous man who supports the Church, ministries to the poor, and other worthwhile charitable organizations. A man who can express love with his money will be capable of really loving you.

## Keeping a balanced perspective on money

"Remove far from me falsehood and lying; give me neither poverty nor riches; feed me with the food that is needful for me, lest I be full, and deny Thee, and say, 'Who is the LORD?' or lest I be poor, and steal, and profane the name of my God" (Proverbs 30:8-9).

Most men find it difficult to keep a balanced perspective on money. In part that's because God calls men to be the main providers in the home. He expects men to work hard, providing for their families as part of their Christian responsibilities. And that means money must become part of their focus.

If you and your husband intend to be generous in the service of life and have a large family, then he needs to be a skilled and industrious worker. You want to find a man who, as the old saying goes, "has found himself and his work" before you marry him. Frequent shifting from job to job and wandering from one career to another often leads to problems in providing.

## Choose a man who will be a good breadwinner

Except for serious health problems, and for temporary arrangements while the husband learns advanced skills to increase his earning potential, it's usually best that the husband not depend upon his wife as the primary breadwinner of the family. Ancient wisdom in the book of Sirach says, "There is wrath and impudence and great disgrace when a wife supports her husband" (25:22). One study found that a $5,000 increase in a wife's earnings after marriage increased the odds of divorce or separation by five percent.[12]

## Priorities and motherhood

Mothers find it extremely difficult to pursue a demanding full-time career outside the home and to nurture children to their potential at the same time. So carefully determine your priorities. Motherhood, especially in a large family, is a full-time, demanding, and yet deeply fulfilling vocation. If you're a woman who intends to join the rapidly growing ranks of mothers leaving the full-time workplace, then you'll have to marry a good provider.

In past generations, a young man spent his teen years preparing for the responsibilities of adulthood. Today, however, the teen years are thought of as a "frozen time" where adult responsibilities are delayed until the next stage of life. Many men don't really "kick into gear" to become good family providers until the first child arrives. This is a late start, especially in our contemporary society, which has eliminated a "family-friendly" economy through its tax and wage structures. In today's economic climate, a wise young man desiring to be a good provider should, throughout the teen years, be developing his ability to provide for a family.

God takes a dim view of a man who doesn't seek to work hard in providing for his family. St. Paul says, "If anyone does not provide for his relatives, and especially for his own family, he has disowned the faith and is worse than an unbeliever" (1 Timothy 5:8).

## Examine a man's priorities

The flip side of this issue is that many men go overboard in the other direction as they turn making a living into an all-consuming desire to make a financial killing. A man with the priorities of money and career first, golf and football second, wife, children and God a distant third, is sure to make a lousy husband. Ask any prospective mate what his life priorities are. If he can't list them, then he isn't ready for marriage. And if his priorities aren't God, family, work—in that order—then keep looking until you find a man with his life in balance. It's *really* worth the wait.

In contrast to the many men overly committed to their work, a somewhat smaller group of men simply lack the necessary motivation and drive to support their families. This type of husband creates such huge levels of frustration in his wife that she frequently seeks an outlet—and often that outlet is divorce or separation.

## Eliminating the risk of marrying an irresponsible provider

How does a young woman know whether a man will turn out to be a good provider? The answer is very simple. Don't court or marry a man until he's demonstrated that he can support a family. This eliminates the risk of marrying first and then merely hoping he'll turn out to be a skilled worker and good provider. Until the disordered days of the late twentieth century, a man never dreamed of seeking a woman's hand in marriage unless he was prepared to demonstrate—to her parents—that he was an able provider.

The book of Proverbs says, "Prepare your work outside, get everything ready for you in the field; and after that build your house" (24:27). Translating this wisdom from an agricultural society to our own, it means, "Get your career and earning potential established first, *then* get married and start your family."

This "get prepared in career before marriage" principle also applies to completing educational and vocational training. Education completed, or nearly completed, before marriage strengthens your relationship. In fact, according to one study, "every year of schooling *before* marriage decreases the likelihood of divorce by about four percent. Yet every year of schooling by husband or wife *after* marriage increases the likelihood of divorce by about six percent."[13]

## Eliminating debt before marriage

While it's prudent to get your education before getting married, it's also wise to get rid of all consumer debt before tying the knot. Starting a family is financially demanding, especially when babies start arriving. A couple should engage in a full and mutual debt disclosure, ideally before publicly announcing an engagement. Each potential spouse needs to list all outstanding debts. Undisclosed debts can be an irritating sore in marriage.

"But we're madly in love, so we can't wait to get married until we pay off our debts!" The Bible says that "love is patient" (1 Corinthians 13:4). The patriarch Jacob worked seven years for each of his two wives. (I don't recommend more than one wife.) The seven years Jacob served for Rachel "seemed to him but a few days because of the love he had for her" (Genesis 29:20).

Your consideration to postpone marriage in order to pay off debts needs to be carefully balanced with concerns for moral purity. Long engagements often carry an increased risk of premarital relations, which weaken faith and family life much more than debts. For that reason, pay attention to the admonition of St. Paul when determining the length of an engagement: "If any one thinks that he is not behaving properly toward his betrothed, if his passions are strong . . . let them marry" (1 Corinthians 7:36).

To have to choose between postponing marriage or entering marriage with debt is less than an ideal situation. As early preparation for successful married life, parents should teach their children the skills needed to escape attachment to material things and the temptation to accumulate debt. Of course, parents need to discover debt-free living for themselves before they can teach these skills to their children.

Regard it as a "red flag" if the man to whom you're considering engagement has piled up considerable debt. No matter what his income potential may be, the jaws of debt will *always* be ready to consume more than he's capable of earning. You want your family to have a solid financial foundation free from the corrosive effects of a lifestyle of unrestrained debt.

Finally, what about college loans? Young couples wanting to enter marriage debt-free but facing $25,000 in college loans for each spouse (which now can be obtained with high-interest credit cards) must give serious thought to how and when those loans will be paid off.

Should most of your college loans be paid off before marriage? Yes, with the exception of loans for a professional degree that provides sufficient earning potential to pay them off within a maximum of seven years. Too many young couples cannot afford both paying off college loans and raising children. And as we'll see in the next section, putting off children for the sake of debt is a shaky way to begin marriage.

## CHAPTER SEVEN

# G

# Generosity in the Service of Life

You must ask yourself a crucial question about your future marriage. Your answer will have profound and lasting effects. Here's the big question: What is the primary purpose of your marriage?

Some possible answers could include highly desirable things: "to love one another for a lifetime"; "to have a soul mate to share life with"; "to share romance"; "to care mutually for each other through all the good times as well as the tough times."

All the above answers are good, but they lack the one chief purpose of marriage that Christians of all centuries until our own have understood—a purpose that's been partially eclipsed in recent generations. In a word, the main purpose of marriage is *kids*. Or to say it the way theologians have for centuries: "The chief end of marriage is the procreation and education of children."

## The secret to fulfilling marital love

I doubt there's a woman reading this book who doesn't want, in the deepest part of her heart, to experience the fullness of love that's possible in Christian marriage. But in order to discover the fullness of marital love, you and your future husband must embrace the secret of the Christian life. Jesus taught that we must lose our lives to find them. He said that the secret to life is not being served, but to serve *others* and to sacrifice for others (see Matthew 10:39; 20:26-28).

Love is elusive. When we seek to receive it more than to give it, love wanes. To experience love in its fullness, you have to go beyond simply seeking to have your need for love met.

Marital love in all its marvelous depth is discovered when it goes outside itself. When a husband and wife through their love bring forth new life, their love is dynamically transformed and enriched. Life-giving love is so potent that it becomes visible—in a new person with an eternal destiny.

An estimated one third of all young couples in our nation today intend to have no more than one child. What a profound mistake to enter marriage with such plans, or even worse, to avoid having children altogether! By willfully rejecting kids, you bottle up precious reserves of love that you'll never savor. (I'm not referring here to those many couples who desire children but can't have them, or who are unable to have all the children they desire. These couples can enrich their marital love by adoption or by special charitable acts to meet the needs of others.)

Yikes! Kids are expensive. They consume your cash, mess up your house, break all your nice stuff, demand all your time, and before leaving home they frequently crash your cars.

Today many young couples reject parenthood with excuses such as these: "We really aren't ready for kids." "We want to advance in our careers, travel to exotic destinations, and have a rich social life together." "We want to be able to afford the better things in life." "Besides, who wants the embarrassment of a screaming brat throwing temper tantrums in the supermarket cereal aisle?" What kind of priorities do such comments reflect?

## Finding happiness in surprising places

What do you want out of marriage? What you really want is to align your marriage as closely as possible to the purposes of God. The closer we align ourselves with our Creator's purposes, the more we find true happiness, fulfillment, and love.

Our Creator seems to have chosen some crazy places to provide fulfillment in marriage: changing messy diapers; sitting up late at night with a sick child; worrying whether the family checkbook will balance with all the bills this month; teaching siblings to get along for the thousandth time. In these challenges, struggles, and sacrifices, however, marital love is most profound, reaching a depth that those in pursuit of personal peace and affluence don't even know exists.

The first words God ever spoke to Adam and Eve were "Be fruitful and multiply" (Genesis 1:28). I know that many modern voices, even some from within the Church, proclaim that this is an outmoded notion. I suggest that you plug your ears to all these anti-life mantras. Instead, heed the voice of God, who hasn't changed His mind about the desirability of children. Jesus still loves the little children very much!

The issue of children is a good subject for a long talk with any prospective husband. Remember, you're not only looking for a good husband for yourself; you're also looking for a good father for your children.

## How many kids?

Many couples want someone to tell them how many kids they should have. But the Church doesn't explicitly insist on a particular number. Instead she encourages all Christian couples to cultivate prayerfully an attitude of generosity in the service of life. Even so, many couples still ask, "How many?"

Let me give you a personal answer. My wife, Karen, and I are the parents of eight children. We've met countless people who go into shock when they see how many children we have. Some think we're freaks for actually wanting so many. We constantly hear comments such as "Are you running a daycare business?" "Haven't you figured out how babies are made yet?" "Are you trying to start a basketball team?"

## What will you say at sixty-five?

Actually, we're just living out Christian family life the way it was designed. I can look anyone straight in the eye and say that I wouldn't change places with any other man in the world. I'm a satisfied man. How many D.I.N.K. (those intentionally choosing "Double Income and No Kids") couples do you know who can say that? How many D.I.N.K. couples will be able to say that when they reach age sixty-five and have a bloated 401(K)—but no grandchildren?

I can't give you a specific number in answer to the "how many kids" question. But the Bible says, "Happy is the man [and woman] who has his quiver full of them!" (Psalm 127:5). How happy and satisfied do you want to be as a result of your sacrifices as a parent?

Once you're married and have a child, pray this prayer a year or two after the birth of each child: "God, do You want us to have one more child? If You do, Lord, please put Your desire in both of our hearts, so that our desires match Your desire." Continue this prayer throughout your childbearing years. You can rest assured of an answer to this prayer. St. Paul wrote, "God is at work in you, both to will and to work for His good pleasure" (Philippians 2:13).

## Let the little children come to Jesus

The *Catechism of the Catholic Church* (hereafter referred to as the *Catechism*) says: "By its very nature the institution of marriage and married love is ordered to the procreation and education of the offspring and it is in them that it finds its crowning glory."[14] Across the centuries Jesus still says to couples today, "Let the children come to me, and do not hinder them; for to such belongs the kingdom of heaven" (Matthew 19:14). Align your future marriage closely with this purpose, and you'll discover all of the mystery of marital love.

## CHAPTER EIGHT

# H

# Honor Your Father and Mother

The book of Genesis describes marriage as a transition from one family to another when it says, "Therefore a man leaves his father and his mother and cleaves to his wife, and they become one flesh" (2:24).

For a successful marriage, both a "leaving" and a "cleaving" have to take place. Your future family naturally grows out of, and in a sense continues, the families you and your future husband grew up in. Besides this healthy continuity, there needs to be a positive transition in which you leave behind the primacy of your birth family relationships in order to start your new family.

Too many couples make the unfortunate mistake of trying to cleave without leaving. No, I'm not talking about the "mama's boy" who can't cut the apron strings. I'm referring to the rebellious, bitter, or ungrateful young person who says, "I can't wait to get out of here. I can't stand my parents, their rules, and their lifestyle."

## Becoming what we focus upon

As we've noted, ironically, such a young person will unwittingly take all his negative family experiences into the new marriage. Instead of a healthy and loving severance of the birth family ties, there will be an ongoing negative focus that binds the new marriage to the past. No matter what our intentions are, we tend to become like what we focus upon. Only healthy separations from the birth family allow for the unencumbered creation of a new family.

## Your "hinge" relationship

Your relationship with your parents is a "hinge relationship" that colors all your other personal relationships. Look at the order of the Ten Commandments: The Fourth Commandment to honor father and mother is the "hinge" between those dealing with the love of God and those dealing with the love of other people. Similarly, your ability to love each other in your marriage is related to how you honor your parents.

St. Paul, repeating the Fourth Commandment, says, "'Honor your father and mother' (this is the first commandment with a promise), 'that it may be well with you and that you may live long on the earth'" (Ephesians 6:2-3). Be hesitant to go forward with a wedding when you don't have your parents' blessing.

## Parental reaction and marital satisfaction

An important study of 5,174 engaged couples found a strong correlation between parental reaction to an upcoming marriage and the satisfaction level of the couple. The figure below shows that when both sets of parents were not in favor of a proposed marriage, about eighty-eight percent of the couples experienced low levels of marital satisfaction.[15] When one set of parents was opposed to the marriage, more than seventy percent experienced low satisfaction.[16]

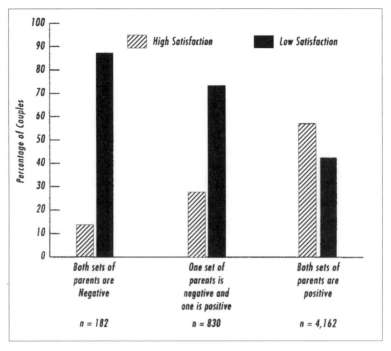

*Marital satisfaction compared with parents' reaction to upcoming marriage*

These data indicate that parents have a good internal warning system about potentially unsatisfying relationships. Seek your parents' guidance, listen to their counsel, and obtain their blessing before setting a wedding date. Your parents' advice, coupled with the insights gleaned from the premarital inventories described in chapter 12, should be heeded if you really want your married life to be happy and satisfying.

## CHAPTER NINE

# I

# Interfaith vs. Same-Faith Marriages

I've heard numerous testimonies from couples in interfaith marriages in which the strong faith of one spouse inspired a conversion experience in the other spouse. Many other interfaith marriages provide opportunities for increased respect, sensitivity, and understanding for each other's beliefs. A number of these couples live happily ever after.

In light of all this, you might ask, "Should I then be unconcerned about faith compatibility in choosing a mate?" To answer that question, you must carefully balance the many stories of successful interfaith marriages against those that didn't end up happily ever after.

## The worst loneliness

Marriage at its best is a sharing of the deepest part of your heart with your husband. The very worst loneliness is the profound sense of isolation many women experience in the midst of their marriages. One frequent cause of this loneliness is a husband unconcerned, uncommitted, and unconnected with the faith of his wife.

Think about what it might be like sitting in a pew without your husband every Sunday morning for the next forty years. Think about never being able to truly share your love for God with your husband. Think about what it might be like never to experience the unifying effect of having you, your husband, and your children praying together.

Do you really want to run such a risk? No wonder St. Paul wisely warns: "Do not be mismated with unbelievers" (2 Corinthians 6:14).

## Why risk incompatibility?

A major reason for writing this book is my strong belief that mountains of marital heartaches (as well as skyrocketing divorce rates) can be dramatically reduced. A shared Christian faith can help you through the turbulent times in marriage. Without a shared belief and value system, you have one more thing to squabble about.

Why run the risk of faith incompatibility? Why choose a marriage in which you're unsure about what his faith will be? The prophet Amos asks: "Can two walk together, except they be agreed" (3:3 KJV)? The hazards stemming from mixed marriages should not be underestimated.

## A threefold cord

A shared faith is the focal point of marital unity. The book of Ecclesiastes says: "Two are better than one, because they have a good reward for their toil. For if they fall, one will lift up his fellow; but woe to him who is alone when he falls and has not another to lift him up. Again, if two lie together, they are warm; but how can one be warm alone? And though a man might prevail against one who is alone, two will withstand him. A threefold cord is not quickly broken" (4:9-12). A shared faith is like the third strand of a threefold cord that binds you and your husband, not only in body and mind, but also in soul.

The children born of your marriage are a principal reason why you want to have a shared faith. While a husband and wife themselves might find equilibrium in an interfaith marriage, a child is liable to be confused or even torn apart by divided loyalties.

## Faith awakening in new parents

To their surprise, many couples have a faith-awakening experience after the birth of their first child. Before becoming parents, your different faiths may not seem like a big deal. Suddenly, you're filled with questions: "Will the baby be baptized?" "In which church will the baby be baptized?" "Where will the child be catechized?" And out of nowhere, you start getting some phone calls from in-laws expressing strong opinions on what should be done.

Faced with such questions, some interfaith couples experience division at a moment when they most need unity. Other interfaith couples try to preserve unity by "agreeing to disagree" about faith questions, or just drop out of church life altogether. They may say, "We'll let the child decide when he becomes an adult."

## Teens and interfaith marriages

A final problem with children in interfaith marriages arises during the teen years. It's hard enough for two parents to guide a teen through adolescence with his faith intact. During most of their childhood, your children may willingly go to church with you every Sunday. But what will you do when they start putting up resistance?

How do you explain to a teen that it's necessary for him to go to church with you, but it's okay for your husband to stay home or to go to another church? How will you dissuade your teenage son from following the example of his father?

The conflicts outlined above are merely potential clashes. They don't automatically occur in interfaith marriages. Many inter-faith couples successfully navigate between these differences without marital discord. But again, why take the risk, especially if your faith is the most meaningful part of your life? Why not marry someone who shares your faith in order to guarantee that you'll at least start your marriage with a common outlook?

God is the best friend that marriage ever had. Don't run the risk of leaving Him out. It's well worth waiting for a man who shares your faith. If he has God at the center of his life, you can't go wrong.

## CHAPTER TEN

# J

# Just How Far Can We Go?

"For everything there is a season, and a time for every matter under heaven: a time to embrace, and a time to refrain from embracing" (Ecclesiastes 3:1,5).

"Okay," you may say, "I'm with you that sexual relations should wait for marriage, as you described in chapter 5. But in the meantime, just how far can we go while waiting for marriage? Isn't kissing and petting okay?"

### The marital embrace is a consuming fire

To answer the kissing and petting question, you need to consider how God designed the marital embrace, along with all the acts leading up to it. He created sex in marriage to be a consuming fire in two respects. First, He made the wonderful flame of the marital embrace itself—a flame that can burn for decades without losing its warmth. Second, once the fire of physical love is intentionally ignited, He's designed it to increase in intensity, until it's fully consummated in the marital embrace.

If you and your boyfriend say that you can fire up steamy passions over an extended period of time and never have problems

49

with serious sexual temptations, then may I suggest a visit to a physician or psychiatrist? Intimate kissing and caressing are designed to ignite the flames of marital love between husband and wife. In creating the great mystery of the marital embrace, God hasn't designed any convenient stopping points on the way to consummated physical love.

## An exhortation from the world's best love song

In the Old Testament, the Song of Songs (also called the Song of Solomon) is an extended love song. The Hebrew title means that it's the greatest of songs. Using the poetic imagery of the passionate love between spouses newly joined in the marriage covenant, the book subtly describes the love between God and His covenant people. The poetic imagery is rich, and much can be gleaned from it.

If you want the best answer to the kissing and caressing question, then listen to the advice at the close of the world's greatest love song: "I adjure you, O daughters of Jerusalem, that you stir not up nor awaken love until it please . . . for love is strong as death . . . Its flashes are flashes of fire, a most vehement flame. Many waters cannot quench love, neither can floods drown it" (8:4, 6-7).

Marital love is something profound, powerful, all-consuming, and sacred. God intended it to consume a man and a woman entirely in the marital embrace. Don't run the risk of stirring it up before marriage.

## Understanding men and sexual temptation

Many women fail to appreciate how easily a man can be aroused. Visual stimuli alone are enough to arouse men; think, then, of what physical touch does to them. A woman may say to herself, "There's no harm in a little kissing," while not realizing that this simple physical stimulus is enough to awaken a strong desire for full sexual expression in a man. The time of kissing ends up either going too far or leaving the man feeling defrauded. Neither of these options is an expression of true love.

## Avoiding regrets

Some people enjoy playing with fire, convinced that they'll never be burned. Yet millions (yes, millions!) of Christian couples intending to remain chaste until marriage have fallen into sexual sin that began with the spark of a little "innocent" kissing. These couples deeply regret that they ever started expressing physical affection before marriage. So why take the risk, especially if you really love someone?

If you deeply love a man and hope to marry him, then you don't want your physical affection to get out of control. Unfortunately, the only way many couples can check their physical desires is to break off the relationship. That's why premarital sex has prematurely ended countless Christian relationships.

## Relationship insurance

Postponing all physical affection until marriage is insurance for a relationship that you really care about. The wisest answer to the "Just how far can we go?" question is: "Zero," "Nada," "Zip." Save *all* the fire for your marriage, and your relationship won't get burned.

Shortly after I first met my wife, Karen, I knew she was someone I was *really* interested in. I wanted our friendship to grow without getting out of hand. So that she didn't think my lack of physical advances stemmed from a lack of interest in her, I suggested that we postpone all physical affection to preserve our special relationship. We never kissed until after she accepted my proposal for marriage.

I thought our waiting to kiss until engaged was really radical back in 1978. But today there are thousands of Christian couples who are taking their relationship insurance a step further. Following the example of couples such as Joshua and Shannon Harris (who have written about their experiences), they're holding off their first kiss until they're declared to be "man and wife."[17] I guarantee that you'll never regret such a wait.

If you need convincing, take a look at the smiling faces and sparkling eyes of the couples who waited for their first kiss at the altar. Instead of fizzling out after a few years, the fires of marital love are blazing in these formerly courting couples. Who would want anything less?

## Help for maintaining your standards

If you agree that the kissing and hugging sessions are off-limits until marriage, you might still wonder, "Where can we find help and encouragement for keeping our commitment?" I repeat my earlier suggestion: Find a "mentoring couple" (see chapter 4) to assist you. An ideal mentoring couple is a husband and wife with a solid marriage who are willing to meet with the two of you at least monthly.

With the increased temptations to intimacy that arise during engagement, you'll probably want to meet weekly, or biweekly, once you're engaged. A wise engaged couple will take this precautionary step to ensure that the first full expression of sexual love is not in sin, but in the sacredness of marital love. Your mentoring couple will help hold you accountable to your standards during courtship and engagement.

If you set the standard of no sexual expression until marriage, then the mentoring couple asks you at each meeting if you've lived up to that standard. It may be just that little bit of help you need to stick to your standards. Like a weekly Weight Watchers meeting where your friends see you step on the scale, accountability helps you pass up tempting choices.

## Short-circuited decision making

There's one final reason why you don't want to arouse your passions before marriage. Deciding to marry someone is the greatest decision you'll make in life. No other decision requires such prudent, prayerful, and careful thinking. But when you fall in love, your romantic emotions alone are enough to take you on a flight above the clouds.

Nevertheless, at no other time in life is it so important that you keep yourself levelheaded. If you overload your emotions with flaming physical passion, your brain's decision-making process will be short-circuited. Rational thought will fly out the window as your passions rule, and the likelihood of making a regrettable marital decision is magnified. You can't be sure of keeping your head if you're involved physically. You could easily be led by your feelings into a lifelong commitment that you may seriously regret.

No wonder St. Paul gave such a stern warning against choosing a spouse in the passions of lust:

"For you know what instructions we gave you through the Lord Jesus. For this is the will of God, your sanctification: that you abstain from immorality; that each one of you know how to control his own body in holiness and honor, not in the passion of lust like heathen who do not know God; that no man transgress, and wrong his brother in this matter, because the Lord is an avenger in all these things, as we solemnly forewarned you" (1 Thessalonians 4:2-6).

You really don't want to have your emotions set on fire with the passion of lust when you're about to make the greatest decision of your life. Don't stir up or awaken physical intimacy until you're married. Once you're married, then you can light that "most vehement flame" of marital love—a love that time will not extinguish.

## CHAPTER ELEVEN

# K

# Know Yourself and Your Future Mate

He's tall, winsome, charming, really good-looking, and agreeable on most everything. He has a great job, and he loves you. What else could you possibly need to know?

Lots! The adage "Marry in haste, repent at leisure," is still true in the twenty-first century. An adrenaline rush to the altar is foolish. Haste to get married is usually infatuation and certainly not genuine love.

While recreational dating lacks any definite aim, the specific purpose of courting is to get to know a man well enough to make a wise choice about marrying him. A prudent decision is made with as much information as possible about yourself and your future mate.

## Gain valuable insights from the family circle

The discernment process begins in your family and in his family. As we've already noted, the imprudent dating patterns of the twentieth century removed courtship from the family circle, with tragic consequences. A wise woman will seek her mother and father's guidance and blessing in each of the various stages in the selection of a marriage partner.

You're shortchanging yourself if you simply bring a prospective mate home for the weekend, announce your engagement, and ask your parents to rubber-stamp your wedding plans. Many heart-wrenching marital mistakes could be avoided if women would enlist their family's aid to gain an honest assessment of the men they're interested in.

One of the unique benefits your family can offer is that they really know you. To make a good marital choice you need to know both yourself and your prospective mate. Often, your family will see things about your relationship that you can't immediately perceive. Be open and attentive to their observations, suggestions, and comments. Allow your family abundant time to get to know the man you're courting.

Likewise, getting to know his parents, siblings, and grandparents will give you insights into who this man is that you're interested in. The generous amount of time you spend with his family, and he with yours, is vital in deciding whether or not to marry.

## Value of marriage preparation

In addition, church-based marriage preparation classes and competent premarital counseling programs can provide valuable assistance in making a good marriage choice. Rather than viewing such programs as obstacles to be overcome on the way to the altar, you should appreciate and eagerly participate in them. Solid marriage preparation classes have demonstrated a wonderful ability to strengthen marriages and lower the probability of divorce.

Such classes will assist you in really getting to know each other. Marital preparation classes will give you penetrating questions to ask each other—questions that you may never have thought of asking. I suggest that you don't publicly announce a wedding date until you've completed *at least* half a marital preparation program.

## Discern before deciding

You want to know as much as possible about yourself and your future mate before making the greatest decision in your life. You want to know as much as you can about his character, religious commitment, disposition, personality type, employment and educational background, health status, and family background. You need to consider if there are any previous marriages; any dependents; present or past addictions; criminal records; credit problems or bankruptcies; psychological or health problems or abusive situations in either of your family backgrounds.

You can avoid these topics, or easily hide them during engagement, but believe me: they will surface in marriage. A good counselor can help the two of you openly discuss and deal with such sensitive issues. Some of these questions take only a few minutes to cover with a counselor, but tackling these topics can prevent decades of heartache.

Unthinkable things happen. I once counseled a woman struggling with marital problems who, after making a few inquiries, found out that her husband was simultaneously married to two other women. Although this discovery went a long way toward explaining the source of her marital difficulties, she would have been better off if she had made her inquiry before marriage.

## Avoid my mistake

I need to tell you about a big mistake I've made in the past when providing premarital counseling. I thought it was sufficient to receive an open acknowledgement of potential problems from a couple after pointing out obvious areas of possible conflict and incompatibility. But I was wrong—in some cases, tragically wrong.

Simply recognizing and admitting a potential source of serious marital conflict is useless unless meaningful action is taken to change it. I naively imagined that an acknowledgement, joined by a serious pledge "to work on it," was enough. But subsequent unhappiness, marital strife, and divorce in the lives of some couples I'd counseled showed me that this wasn't enough. Real action with substantial evidence of improvement *before* marriage was needed. Why risk entering into marriage unless significant change has already taken place and potentially serious sources of marital strife have been removed?

## What you see is what you get

As the president of a nonprofit organization, I've had to learn an important principle for good hiring that you can use in choosing a husband as well. I've found that in ninety-nine percent of employment decisions, "What You See Is What You Get" (WYSIWYG).

As an employer, I've made the mistake of imagining that an employee would function as I would if I were in that particular position. But people are very likely to function in a new position much as they have functioned in the past, especially in the recent past. I've had to curb my personal projections about what a person *might* do, and instead carefully observe what he was *actually* doing.

The same is true in choosing a husband: You need to see how he is now in real life, not how you imagine him to be in a blissful romantic fantasy of a future marriage. If you really don't like what you see now, then don't marry the man.

Don't think that a wedding ceremony followed by a few months of goading will change your husband. Personality traits, levels of motivation, personal and family habits, character, interests, temperament, and life priorities are not magically transformed by walking down an aisle. Remember WYSIWYG!

No, you don't have to find Mr. Perfect. He doesn't exist, and you don't have the right to demand perfection unless you happen to fall into that category yourself. But you should have a clear idea of who it is you're marrying, and especially take note of any character defects you would find impossible to live with. If you've done your homework, then you'll never have to lament, "Oh, if only I had known."

## The time for commitment

If, after a sufficient time to get to know each other's character, disposition, and background, you like what you've learned, and if you've obtained good premarital counseling and your parents' blessings, then go ahead and make your decision. At this point, a man should be willing to express his intention for marriage, and you should be ready to give him a response. There's no need to prolong your engagement unduly after this point without a strong, mutually-agreed-upon reason to do so. Just go into marriage with your eyes wide open.

## CHAPTER TWELVE

# L

# Love is Blind—but Premarital Inventories Aid Sight Recovery

Infatuation and emotional love may be blind, but you shouldn't be. Be sure to utilize resources that will help give you 20/20 vision before deciding upon a life partner.

Premarital inventories, such as PREPARE and FOCCUS, have stunning track records in predicting the probabilities of marital success or failure. While some of these inventories resist describing themselves as predictive instruments, both FOCCUS and PREPARE have high levels of reliability verified by third-party follow-up studies, and they are among the best of the premarital inventories. FOCCUS was found to predict high-quality versus low-quality relationships with eighty to eighty-two percent reliability. PREPARE has demonstrated an ability to distinguish couples who eventually get divorced from those who remain happily married, with eighty to eighty-five percent accuracy.

These are astonishing results. If you're serious about getting assistance in discerning a potentially high-risk relationship, or a potentially successful one, then the modest amount of time and money required for an assessment such as FOCCUS or PREPARE is a smart investment in your future.

One strong caution about exaggerated expectations from these inventories: sometimes unwarranted assumptions and excessive dependencies are attributed to them. These inventories are *not* pass-or-fail tests. They don't make any claim to give an infallible prediction about any single relationship. A premarital inventory should not be used as the sole criterion in making a marriage decision.

The purpose of premarital inventories is to point out areas of both strength and challenge. Their special value extends far beyond the actual assessment, especially in the way they often spark deeper levels of communication, problem-solving, and clear-headed thinking. Using a premarital inventory can help you start talking about some topics that you may have been avoiding. Inventories cover areas such as finances, role relations, in-laws, leisure, sex, communication, and conflict resolution.

## FOCCUS
## Facilitating Open Couple Communication, Understanding, and Study

3214 N. 60th St., Omaha, NE 68104

1-888-874-2684; www.foccusinc.com

FOCCUS was developed by experienced marriage and family counselors through the Family Life Office in Omaha, Nebraska. FOCCUS, while covering the same wide range of topics as other inventories, includes an important spiritual component. Since studies show that couples with a strong faith life in their marriage are more stable and satisfied in their relationships, it makes lots of sense to include spirituality in a premarital inventory— especially for Christians. FOCCUS is offered in four editions, including a Christian nondenominational edition and a Catholic edition.

FOCCUS, like PREPARE, can be used for those seriously considering marriage as well as those who are already engaged. (There is also a REFOCCUS marital inventory available to couples wishing to improve their relationship in their existing marriage.)

FOCCUS is very affordable. I can't think of a single reason why every about-to-be-engaged, or already-engaged, couple would not want to take the FOCCUS inventory.

## PREPARE
P.O. Box 190, Minneapolis, MN 55440
1-800-331-1661; www.prepare-enrich.com

More than a million couples have taken PREPARE (for premarital couples) and ENRICH (for married couples). The inventory's goal is to assess and explore your relationship's strengths as well as areas needing growth. Couples take a 195-question inventory to help prepare them for marriage and to enrich their relationship.

The PREPARE inventory, like FOCCUS, has high levels of reliability, verified through follow-up studies. PREPARE offers excellent materials for couples as a way of following up on the discoveries made when taking the inventory.

Either one of these inventories will provide a valuable assessment of your relationship. I think you'd be wise to take one of these inventories before making your decision to get engaged. If you're already engaged, then by all means take the inventory *before* publicly setting a wedding date.

Remember, these inventories do not and cannot make any marital decision for you. Their value is in giving you a clearer picture of your relationship, and based on that, *you* can make a better-informed decision.

My only criticism of PREPARE and FOCCUS is that they are priced too economically. I'm afraid that their low price might suggest a low worth to some couples. I'd still recommend these instruments even if they cost as much as a wedding cake. When you consider that they cost only a tiny fraction of what most couples spend on their cake, there's no excuse for not taking advantage of them.

This may not be earth-shaking news to women, but many men aren't excited about going to premarital classes. Yet follow-up studies of premarital classes have reported that men like the inventories better than any other part of the classes. Tuck this fact away in case you need encouragement for your man because he's dragging his heels over joining a marriage preparation class.

## Premarital inventories accelerate relationships

Taking one of these inventories is an eye-opening experience for couples contemplating marriage. The process will either accelerate the development of your relationship or accelerate its breakup. About ten percent of those taking PREPARE or a similar inventory end up postponing or breaking off their engagement, or even ending their relationship.

You might react to this statistic by saying, "I don't want anything to do with these things!" or asking, "Why should I jeopardize my engagement?" The answer is twofold.

First, while these instruments result in some couples breaking off their engagement, many others find their relationships greatly strengthened because they go on to explore the findings of the inventories with each other and with a counselor.

Second, you don't need to take a blind leap to enter marriage. Many young women are avoiding marriage altogether because they're scared of falling into an ocean of divorce-inflicted heart-breaks. These instruments will help you see what you're getting into. Again, they don't give any absolute guarantee, but they can certainly help you know yourself and your potential spouse more accurately.

The decision to marry is still one hundred percent yours to make, but the premarital inventories will assist you in making a wiser marriage decision. Take your close look now. Then once you're married, you'll never need to look back.

## Your decision comes before setting the date

Never set a wedding date (or at least don't publicly announce a wedding date and begin making wedding plans) before fully determining if a particular man should be your mate. Prematurely setting a wedding date shuts down the decision-making process and sets you up for getting pressured into a marriage you may feel uncomfortable about.

Before setting a wedding date, you need competent counsel from your family, your church, or marriage counselors. I personally refuse to start premarital counseling with couples who have announced a wedding date. Once the date is set and announced, the big decision about whom to marry is eclipsed by decisions about things such as bridesmaids, dresses, florists, photographers, cake, invitations, and a thousand other concerns.

While many couples regard joining a premarital program as a certain step toward marriage, you should consider the final decision an open question until you've completed at least half a premarital program and have taken either the FOCCUS or PRE-PARE inventories.

## CHAPTER THIRTEEN

# M

# Marriage is a Sacrament—a Mystery of Grace and Love

A re you interested in discovering some astonishingly good news about the mystery of marital love? Do you want to experience a depth of love that's beyond anything a romance novel has ever suggested? If your answer is yes, then I suggest that you read this chapter slowly and carefully.

## The Trinity and the sacrament of marriage

At the heart of the universe is the Blessed Trinity. A fire of divine love radiates between the three persons of the Trinity. The intensity of this divine love burns brighter than the sun. The *Catechism* says: "The mystery of the Most Holy Trinity is the central mystery of Christian faith and life. It is the mystery of God in Himself. It is therefore the source of all the other mysteries of faith, the light that enlightens them."[18]

The Trinity holds the secret to the depths of love possible in the sacrament of marriage. You were made to know and experience the love of God. God has placed the deepest yearning inside you to be joined as an adopted daughter of the Blessed Trinity. By baptism in Christ, you were joined in a family bond, a covenant, with God as your Father, with Jesus as your covenant brother, and with the Holy Spirit.

When a baptized man and a baptized woman with their free consent bind themselves together for life in a lawful marriage, they enter the sacrament of Matrimony. The *Baltimore Catechism* defines a sacrament as "an outward sign instituted by Christ to give grace." This grace unites us to Christ and the entire Trinity in a covenant bond of love.

## The fire of divine love in your marriage

The flame of divine love within the Blessed Trinity is imparted in a special way to a man and a woman joined in the sacrament of marriage. As Moses was told to remove his shoes before the burning bush because he was standing on holy ground, so with reverence are we to regard the sacrament of marriage as a holy and sacred dwelling where the fires of divine charity burn.

God is willing to enkindle the deepest of affections between you and your future husband in the sacrament of marriage. The fire of divine charity from within the heart of the universe, the Blessed Trinity, can be in your heart, your husband's heart, and in the heart of your marriage. The deepest affections of your hearts can be ablaze with heavenly grace.

St. Paul says that the very love with which Christ loves the Church is mysteriously present in the New Covenant sacrament of marriage (see Ephesians 5). In the New Covenant, Christ has elevated the good of natural marriage to incredible heights. He made Matrimony a sacrament and He has taken marriage into Himself.

## Expression of heartfelt affection

How might this vision of the sacrament of marriage be expressed to you by your future husband? St. John Chrysostom, commenting on Ephesians 5, suggests that young Christian husbands should say to their wives: "I have taken you in my arms, and I love you, and I prefer you to my life itself. For the present life is nothing, and my most ardent dream is to spend it with you in such a way that we may be assured of not being separated in the life reserved for us. . . . I place your love above all things."[19]

## What happened to marriage?

What in the world has happened to marriage? Instead of this exalted view of a marvelous Christian sacrament, we're more likely to see marriages resembling a defective booster rocket: They fire up, blast off, spin out of control, and land not long afterwards with a crash and burn.

Many reasons can be given for the current pitiful state of marriage, but one particular reason is generally neglected by social scientists. Around the time of the Protestant Reformation, Christian marriage was explicitly denied by the Reformers to be a sacrament. They still held it to be an important divine institution, but they unfortunately declared that it was essentially a civil union.

With the rapid rise of many of the new nation-states, primary jurisdiction over marriage was transferred from Church to state, and marriage itself was devalued from a sacrament to a civil contract.[20] It took a few hundred years for the effects of this switch to work their way into society. But today we see the ripe fruits of the change in drive-through weddings, instant no-fault divorces, and soaring divorce rates—even among Christians.

## The ultimate renewal of marriage

Many noble and extremely well-intentioned efforts are under way today to reform civil marriage. Such efforts, while commendable, can only go so far. Marriage as a civil institution is essentially a breakable contract. In the near future, the state will probably view marriage as a breakable contract simply between two persons, not necessarily a man and woman. While we assuredly can reduce a good deal of the runaway rate of marital breakup through civil reforms, we cannot really heal the heart of Christian marriage without a conscious return to the sacrament of marriage.

So what will you do? I can't imagine a Christian of any denominational background reading this chapter and not wanting to experience all the sacramental blessings of marriage. You and your future husband will want to enter marriage with a full conviction that it's a sacrament. To bolster your understanding, I encourage reading (and meditating) on the subject of marriage from Christian traditions that have continuously honored it as a sacrament. A reliable and readable introduction to the sacrament of marriage can be found in the *Catechism* (see par. 1601–1666).

The civil government can give you a marriage certificate, and a divorce later on if things don't go well. Christ, by elevating marriage to a sacrament, can give you and your future spouse special, long-lasting marital graces that will inflame your covenant union with divine love.

## An often overlooked resource for the sacrament of marriage

Pope Pius XI, describing the graces available in the sacrament of marriage, had this to say:

The grace of matrimony will remain for the most part an unused talent hidden in the field unless the parties exercise these supernatural powers and cultivate and develop the seeds of grace they have received. If, however, doing all that lies within their power, they cooperate diligently, they will be able with ease to bear the burdens of their state and to fulfill their duties.

An oft-repeated consideration of their state of life, and a diligent reflection on the sacrament they have received, will be of great assistance to them. Let them constantly keep in mind, that they have been sanctified and strengthened for the duties and for the dignity of their state by a special sacrament, the efficacious power of which . . . is undying.

Let not, then, those who are joined in matrimony neglect the grace of the sacrament which is in them; for, in applying themselves to the careful observance . . . of their duties they will find the power of that grace becoming more effectual as time goes on.[21]

For lasting love you'll need a constant source of strength invigorating your marriage. For those Christian couples who are careful to appropriate them, the sacramental graces of Matrimony bring the fires of divine love from the Blessed Trinity into the heart of their marriage. This is one treasure you don't want to neglect in your marriage. Why not start now to develop your appreciation and understanding of the sacrament of marriage?

## CHAPTER FOURTEEN

# N

# Narcissistic Men

The very last person you want to select as a husband is a narcissistic man. The self-centered, self-absorbed, and self-admiring man is searching for a trophy wife to orbit his over-sized ego, and you don't want to be that woman.

## Men in love with themselves

Why do women so often fall for men stuck on themselves? It's easy to understand why a woman would be attracted to a man with above-average athletic ability, good looks, intelligence, or income-earning ability. Yet these are the types of men most prone to fall in love with themselves.

Men of humble circumstances are certainly liable to self-love. But men blessed with an exceptional amount of brains, brawn, or wealth are easy prey in the clutches of narcissism. Even if a narcissistic man is loaded with money, smarts, or good looks, unhappiness waits for the woman foolish enough to marry him.

## Greater gifts require greater grace

If you're considering marriage to a man with great gifts, then make sure he avails himself of greater measures of grace. The book of Sirach says, "The greater you are, the more you must humble yourself; so you will find favor in the sight of the Lord" (3:18).

God commanded the ancient Israelite kings to read God's word every day so their hearts would not be lifted up in pride over their brethren (see Deuteronomy 17:18-20). He warned all the Israelites to remember to thank God when they experienced prosperity (see Deuteronomy 8:10-18). When gold and silver increase, so does the propensity for pride that leads to forgetfulness of God. For that reason, God commanded an increase in thanksgiving as prosperity increased. These exhortations to the ancient Israelites are good reminders for all Christians who want to master their pride.

Men deprived of stable family life and two loving parents may also be prone to excessive self-love. The early years of family life are critical in helping a boy mature beyond childish self-centeredness into a man capable of self-giving love. A dysfunctional family environment can arrest this process of maturation.

I'm not implying here that every young man from a dysfunctional family, or who is exceptionally talented or good-looking, will be narcissistic. You just need to keep your personal "radar warning system" functioning so you can avoid getting entangled with someone who's just an oversized boy. Instead, you want to marry a mature man capable of loving you.

## Determining what lies at the core of a man

St. Augustine said in his book *The City of God* that humanity is divided into two "cities." The first "city," the city of the world, is fixated on a love of self. This is the condition of people unchanged by God's saving grace in Christ. In contrast is the second "city," the city of God, characterized by a love for both God and neighbor.

While everyone struggles with a tendency toward self-centeredness, some people have enthroned their own egos in their hearts. So you need to determine what lies at the core of the man you're interested in. Does he live in the city of the world or the city of God? Is his fundamental life-orientation self-centered or God-centered? Is the self enthroned in his heart, or is Jesus Christ?

If selfishness rules him, he won't be able to offer the self-giving love every woman wishes for in marriage—unless he has a spiritual conversion. A new life in Christ entails a death to our old ego and a rebirth with Christ living, reigning, and loving from the center of our life. St. Paul described this ego transformation in his own life this way: "I have been crucified with Christ; it is no longer I who live, but Christ who lives in me; and the life I now live in the flesh I live by faith in the Son of God, who loved me and gave himself for me" (Galatians 2:20).

A man transformed by grace, who loves God and his neighbor, is the kind of man you want pledging lifelong love to you.

## CHAPTER FIFTEEN

# O

# Occasional Fights Are Okay—*Really*!

You and your fiancé just had a big blowup, so now you're thinking about breaking off your engagement. With profound disillusionment you're saying to yourself, "If two people really loved each other, they would never have a fight like we had."

Slow down. A fight doesn't necessarily mean you should break an engagement or end a relationship.

## Targeting problems rather than each other

If you've had a fight and were able to identify and target the problem causing friction between the two of you, rather than just blasting each other, then you're far better prepared for a lasting marriage than a couple who has never fought. So don't break off your engagement just because you had a heated argument. What you do need is to learn conflict resolution skills to deal with the inevitable differences that arise in marriage.

You need to know three facts about marital and premarital fights. First, *all* married couples fight, even though many couples fail to admit it. At a recent conference for Christian husbands and fathers, I asked the two hundred men in attendance, "How many of you have fights with your wife?" About a dozen men raised their hands. I told the rest of the men that they might need to go to confession for being less than truthful.

## The number-one predictor of divorce

Second, just because you fight doesn't mean that your marriage will be doomed. In fact, the opposite may be true. Secular marriage research has found the habitual *avoidance* of conflict is the number-one predictor of divorce. Amazingly, the couples who stay married don't have fewer differences or fights than couples who divorce. Both sets of couples disagree about the same types of things (money, kids, sexual relations, housework, in-laws). The big difference between the two groups of couples is *how* they handle their disagreement. For instance, biting sarcasm and stonewalling during arguments are high predictors of divorce.

## Taming the tongue

Third, remember that a great way to prevent conflicts, or to heal ones already under way, is to tame the tongue. Jesus taught us to pray: "Lead us not into temptation" (Matthew 6:13). Since the tongue so often leads the way into discord, it's wise for every Christian couple to pray daily for control of the tongue. The words of Psalm 19:14 form a short yet effective prayer for control of the tongue: "Let the words of my mouth and the meditation of my heart be acceptable in thy sight, O LORD, my rock and my redeemer."

If an argument erupts, but it's still in the early "flaring up" stage, remember a couple of verses from Proverbs that can come to your rescue:

"A soft answer turns away wrath, but a harsh word stirs up anger" (Proverbs 15:1).

"There is one whose rash words are like sword thrusts, but the tongue of the wise brings healing" (Proverbs 12:18).

Real married life, engagements, courtships, and even honeymoons have occasional fights. Such times, though trying, aren't signs of the end of your relationship. They are actually opportunities for deepening your love, strengthening your communication, and learning the meaning of the twelve most important words for family life spoken by Jesus: "Forgive us our trespasses, as we forgive those who trespass against us" (see Matthew 6:12).

In the aftermath of a fight, apologize and ask for forgiveness. Do this every time. "Honey, I'm sorry for . . . . Will you forgive me?" It's not enough to say you're sorry. You must also seek reconciliation and forgiveness.

## CHAPTER SIXTEEN

# P

# Pray for a Good Husband

Dave, a senior at the Franciscan University of Steubenville, sensed that the time was right to begin seeking a wife. He went to the campus chapel and prayed in the presence of the Blessed Sacrament for a life partner. Just then, Trina, also a senior, decided to make a prayer visit to the chapel on her way from the library back to her dorm.

As Dave was leaving the chapel, he met Trina. Although they had seen each other on campus, this was the first time they really met and stopped to talk. I'm sure Dave wasn't expecting such a quick answer to his prayers for a wife, but that's what happened. Dave and Trina were married eighteen months later. They are now the parents of a beautiful little girl.

We can reverently pray anywhere, at anytime, and expect God to hear our prayer. Yet St. John's Gospel clearly indicates a special context for effectual prayer. In the very process of instituting the Blessed Sacrament during the Last Supper, Jesus said: "Whatever you ask in my name, I will do it, that the Father may be glorified in the Son; if you ask anything in my name, I will do it" (John 14:13-14). A special dynamism takes place when you present your prayer requests for a good husband to God the Father in the name of Jesus while in the presence of the Blessed Sacrament (see also John 15:7, 16:23-24).

Jesus taught us to pray for *all* our needs, not just those items we might regard as "spiritual." For instance, in the "Our Father," Jesus taught us to pray to our heavenly Father for things as basic as daily bread. Certainly, then, praying for a good Christian husband should not be outside the scope of your prayer life.

You don't have to fear being honest with God when praying for a spouse. He already knows the deepest thoughts and desires of your heart. If you're anxious about finding a mate, then "cast all your anxieties on Him, for He cares about you" (1 Peter 5:7).

## Turning cares into prayers

It's wisely said that the best cure for anxiety is to turn your cares into prayers. St. Paul insisted: "Have no anxiety about anything, but in everything by prayer and supplication with thanksgiving let your requests be made known to God. And the peace of God, which passes all understanding, will keep your hearts and your minds in Christ Jesus" (Philippians 4:6-7).

Since you are to pray "Thy will be done," you should ask God to reveal His will for a spouse. Ask Jesus, the Good Shepherd, to direct your steps in fulfilling His will. Keep before you Scripture verses for guidance such as these:

"Trust in the LORD with all your heart, and do not rely on your own insight. In all your ways acknowledge Him, and He will make straight your paths" (Proverbs 3:5-6).

"Teach me to do Thy will, for Thou art my God! Let Thy good spirit lead me on a level path" (Psalm 143:10).

Just in case someone reading this book needs to hear this admonition, I should note that horoscopes are highly displeasing to God and are a sinful way to seek guidance. Turning to horoscopes is turning away from trust in God.

## Lead us not into disastrous decisions

Prayer for guidance also means asking for God's help in not being led into temptation. Ask God to keep you from making a catastrophic decision. Ask for protective guidance from your guardian angel and from St. Raphael.

The archangel Raphael in the Old Testament book of Tobit disguised himself as a traveling companion of Tobias. (The book of Tobit is not found in Protestant Bibles, but it's in the Septuagint, the Greek edition of the Old Testament used by St. Paul and the early Church, and it's been in the Catholic Bible ever since.) St. Raphael provided protection and guidance for Tobias on his way to meet and marry Sarah. You too should ask for the assistance of this archangel, who is the patron of engaged couples.

## Pray for your future husband

Right now, you can start praying for your future husband. Even though you may have no idea who your husband will be, God certainly knows. A good Christian friend of mine, J. P., told me that he credits his avoiding the many moral pitfalls in college and in the military to the prayers of his wife, Louise, long before they even met. J. P. looked me in the eye and said, "Where I am today as a Christian is because of her prayers for me before we ever came together." Before they were married, Louise had been asking for the intercession of Mary to protect her future husband.

## Asking the Holy Family to pray for you

The Bible says, "The prayer of a righteous man [or woman] has great power in its effects" (James 5:16). Certainly, Mary, Jesus' mother, and Joseph, the foster-father of Jesus, are the righteous saints closest to Jesus who can intercede with their Son on your behalf. In fact, you should seek the prayer assistance of the entire Holy Family (Jesus, Mary, and Joseph) as you seek to start your family.

When you pray, ask for a few ounces of patience. Patience allows us to avoid panicking about a spouse and settling for second best. Wait for God to give you the incomparable gift of a good spouse.

## A love story from Genesis

One of the greatest marriage stories in the Bible is that of Isaac and Rebekah in Genesis chapter 24. The patriarch Abraham, an earthly reflection of the heavenly Father, sends his servant out to a distant country to find and bring a bride home to his son Isaac. Through a series of providential events, the servant meets Rebekah and is introduced to her family.

Rebekah, with her family's blessing, consents to go with the servant to marry Isaac. Talk about trusting God for a spouse! Rebekah was willing to marry Isaac sight unseen.

In the meantime, Isaac was back home watching his father's flock. One evening Isaac went out into the field to meditate. Just then the servant and Rebekah approached from a distance.

What would this first meeting be like? Would Rebekah be disappointed in the man that Divine Providence was leading her to? Not at all!

The Bible says, "Rebekah lifted up her eyes, and when she saw Isaac, she alighted from the camel, and said to the servant, 'Who is the man yonder, walking in the field to meet us?' The servant said, 'It is my master'" (Genesis 24:64-65). Isaac and Rebekah had been destined for each other, yet only now would they have the thrill of meeting. I've had one unforgettable experience of riding a camel, and it seems to me that a person would have to be highly excited to "alight from a camel." Rebekah was obviously taken when she saw Isaac, the man God had prepared for her.

The Bible says, "Take delight in the LORD, and He will give you the desires of your heart" (Psalm 37:4). You can trust God, as Rebekah did, to give you the desires of your heart.

## A secret to divine guidance

You should keep in mind this secret to divine guidance: I've found that God's gracious hand often acts after we've served others. Isaiah chapter 58 is the clearest Scripture passage teaching this principle:

> Is not this the fast that I choose: to loose the bonds of wickedness, to undo the thongs of the yoke, to let the oppressed go free, and to break every yoke? Is it not to share your bread with the hungry, and bring the homeless poor into your house; when you see the naked, to cover him, and not to hide yourself from your own flesh? **Then shall your light break forth like the dawn**, and your healing shall spring up speedily; your righteousness shall go before you, the glory of the LORD shall be your rear guard. **Then you shall call, and the LORD will answer; you shall cry, and He will say, Here I am.** If you take away from the midst of you the yoke, the pointing of the finger, and speaking wickedness, if you pour yourself out for the hungry and satisfy the desire of the afflicted, then shall your light rise in the

darkness and your gloom be as the noonday. **And the LORD will guide you continually, and satisfy your desire with good things** (Isaiah 58:6-11, emphasis added).

When I was seeking a wife, I frequently thought about Isaiah 58 and Genesis 24. With expectant hope (and a few anxieties), I trusted that God would bring the right woman into my life. At the time, I was engaged in a challenging youth ministry. My expectation was that God would take care of my needs if I busied myself in shepherding the teens under my care.

I met my wife, Karen, right in the middle of the church building where I conducted my youth ministry. God providentially brought Karen all the way from New York to a Florida youth ministry so we could meet and get married. It took me very little time to realize that God exceeded all my hopes, expectations, and prayers in bringing Karen into my life.

Someone has said that it's difficult to steer a docked boat. A boat needs to be moving before the rudder can guide its course. In the same way, you'll most likely find God's guidance as you serve wholeheartedly at the tasks He's called you to.

Don't just stay at home hoping for a husband to drop down the chimney. Serve at conferences, in your church, in a catechism class, in a youth group, in a pro-life group, or in a community group. Give primacy to serving the needs of others. Pray—especially in the presence of the Blessed Sacrament.

Ask others to pray. Ask for the intercession of the saints and for the guidance of the angels. Finally, trust that God will answer your prayers and give you a good man.

"The LORD is near to all who call upon Him, to all who call upon Him in truth. He fulfils the desire of all who fear Him" (Psalm 145:18-19).

## CHAPTER SEVENTEEN

# Q

# Questions to Ask Before Saying, "I Do"

Pick up a book with a title such as *How to Interview Anyone* or *The Secrets to Dynamic Conversation,* and you'll find that good questions are the keys to unlocking the mind and heart of even the most guarded person. Asking good questions of a prospective husband is an excellent way to get to know him, as well as his plans and expectations for married life.

Before asking the deep, probing questions, it's generally best to start with comfortable openers such as "What's your favorite flavor of ice cream?" or "What are your favorite outdoor activities?" In time, you'll be ready to move on to deeper topics. More sensitive topics, such as health status, previous marriages, possible dependents, addictions, criminal record, bankruptcies, psychological treatments, and abusive family situations, might best be asked by a marriage counselor or pastor.

Here's a sample list of questions you can use in conversation. You'll see some similar questions on the FOCCUS and PRE-PARE instruments. You can easily think up at least a few dozen more questions to ask. Don't just daydream and wonder about what a man thinks. Ask him!

### "What are your favorites?"

What are your favorite foods?

What are your favorite sports?

What are your favorite teams? Do you get to attend games often?

What is your favorite type of music?

What are your favorite books?

What are your favorite TV shows?

What are your favorite movies?

What are your favorite things to do on a vacation?

What is your idea of an ideal weekend?

### Family background

What are some of your best family memories from childhood?

How did your family celebrate the holidays?

Did your family move much during your childhood?

What kind of relationship do you have with your mother and father?

What is your parents' marriage like?

### Attitudes about children

Have you spent any time around young children over the past several years?

Do you like being around children?

Do you think daycare is a good idea for young children?

What do you think is the ideal number of children in a family?

What type of education would you want for your children (public, private, parochial, homeschool)?

Would you want your children to attend college? Any particular colleges?

### Child-rearing and discipline

How did your parents discipline you as a child?

What type of child discipline do you believe in?

Have you read any books or listened to tapes on child discipline?

Who do you feel should be primarily responsible for a child's discipline: the father or the mother?

## Work and family finances

What jobs have you held?

Do you like your work?

What are your thoughts on a mother working outside the home?

Would you take a job or a promotion that required extensive travel away from your family?

If you received a $100,000 inheritance, what would you do with it?

What types of things are you willing to go into debt for?

What are acceptable levels of family debt?

Do you give to religious and other charitable concerns?

## The future and family life

Do you have desires or plans for any further career, college, or graduate education?

What type of work would you like to be doing ten years from now?

Where would you expect to celebrate Thanksgiving and Christmas (and other holidays) after you're married?

## Practicing the Faith

Do you have any type of daily prayer or devotions, such as reading the Bible?

Would you want your family to pray together?

Which religious leaders do you look up to?

Do you take any exceptions to the moral teaching of the Church?

What do you think about men occasionally viewing pornography online?

## CHAPTER EIGHTEEN

# R

# Romeo Online

New technology can spark courtship correspondence. Expanding railroads and improved roads in the nineteenth century provided speedier mail service. Courtship correspondence flourished as a result of these technological improvements. The golden age of American courtship correspondence was from about 1800 to 1880.

During this golden age, couples wrote to each other frequently—sometimes after only a few hours apart. Courtship correspondence was an invaluable means of both establishing and deepening relationships. Perhaps to the surprise of most women today, men did the lion's share of letter writing during this period.

Correspondence was a valuable part of courtship for two particular reasons. First, writing each other allowed couples to get better acquainted without endangering their relationship with excessive physical intimacy—a difficult balancing act in every generation. Second, men weren't ashamed to express themselves in warm, romantic, and heartfelt ways. Here's just one line from a letter in 1808 that an eligible woman in any generation would enjoy receiving: "Excepting my obligation to God, my heart, my affections, my undivided and unreserved love are yours."[22]

Ecclesiastes says, "What has been is what will be, and what has been done is what will be done; and there is nothing new under the sun" (1:9). With the technological advances of the Internet and e-mail, romances developed through online correspondence are flourishing. It seems as though history is indeed repeating itself.

Given this situation, two characteristics from the golden age of courtship correspondence should be brought forward to the twenty-first century. First, letters of that period were phrased with great diligence. Correspondence was polished before being written with the finest penmanship. The slang and broken grammar used with AOL's Instant Messenger is fine for fun and informal online chatter, but we also need to use e-mail to correspond with deeper and more thoughtful letters.

## Expressing affections online

The second characteristic needing resurrection from the golden age of correspondence is that men of that time were romantically expressive in their letters. In fact, many women during this period felt that correspondence brought out more of a man's inner soul than face-to-face conversations. I think they were correct. In fact, they may have made the greatest discovery since Columbus arrived in the New World: courtship correspondence seemed to bring out the best in men, especially helping them overcome that perpetual difficulty in expressing themselves verbally to their fiancés and wives.

It's tough for most guys to communicate what they feel for their wives. I realize that you find this verbal paralysis somewhat incomprehensible, but it's true. Mustering the courage to write love letters online during courtship will help men to express love verbally in marriage.

## The three little words

Today, many men literally can't bring themselves to write three little words, "I love you," on a Valentine's Day card. Millions of other men find it impossible to look their wives in the eye and say, "I love you." For those of you who don't believe this, next Valentine's Day carefully read the dozens of cards that men purchase saying something like this: "For all the times I wanted to say I love you but didn't . . . I am giving you this card."

Nice touch in a card, but not sufficient verbal expression for the vast majority of wives. The guy whose communication skills are stretched by saying, "Whassup!" on Instant Messenger isn't the guy who will satisfy your heart in marriage.

## Prime time to develop communication skills

The courting period is the prime time for men to develop their relational communication skills. Your husband's verbal communication in marriage will usually not rise above the level it reaches during courtship, unless intervention and training take place (such as what we do in our St. Joseph's Covenant Keepers conferences). So give gentle encouragement to the Romeo in the man you're courting. Let him know that you're excited to hear, "You've got mail!" Give a few hints that you appreciate online love letters.

## Questions and answers—an easy way to get to know each other

In your online courtship correspondence, you can use e-mail to send questions such as the list of suggestions in the previous chapter for getting better acquainted. Just don't scan and send all the questions at one time! That could be a bit overwhelming, and it would resemble an interrogation more than communication. Just allow one question and answer to lead naturally to another related, and perhaps deeper, question.

## Online precautions

While I'm enthusiastic about online romance, I urge you to take the strongest possible precautions when you meet someone online. As a young woman, you need to avoid about ninety percent of online chatrooms. You should be extremely cautious about giving out any personal information online. I suggest that you meet your Romeo online in a monitored Christian site that requires documented identification (photo I.D., driver's license, credit card, listed phone number).

Even these Christian sites are not fail-safe. I've read reports of people hiding personal information, making misleading statements, and even outright lying on some Christian singles sites. A Christian site requiring registration will eliminate ninety-five percent of the horde of Internet riff-raff that you want to avoid. Yet, you still need to practice discernment at any singles site. For a list of some good Christian Web sites requiring documented identification, visit our Web site, www.familylifecenter.net, and click on "Courtship."

## Dads and daughters practicing courtship in cyberspace

A timeless courtship principle is to honor your parents. For a young woman especially, this includes honoring your father's role as guardian and loving leader of the family. How do you practice family-centered courtship practices in cyberspace?

Here's how the principle of involving your parents might work in cyberspace. Suppose you get an e-mail from a man who's a member of an online singles community you've joined. He asks for your permission to correspond with you.

You immediately reply with an e-mail thanking him for contacting you. In your initial reply you graciously inform him that any man who wishes to start corresponding with you has first to obtain permission from your father (or your brother, grandfather, uncle or other family member if your father is deceased). Give him your father's e-mail address (or physical address, if your dad is not online yet). Suggest that his e-mail contain his request and a little description of himself and his family.

You and your father have worked out an arrangement in advance of this situation. If he gets any request, he doesn't reply before contacting you. If you look up this man's profile posted on the community bulletin board and don't care for what you see, then just tell your dad.

As we noted before, so many women get involved with guys they know aren't for them simply because they find it difficult to say no. Since you've started your correspondence with your father in the loop, you can easily bring him in at any time if inappropriate communications begin, or if you think it's time to stop the online correspondence. Let your dad help you.

Now let's assume that you look up the man's online profile and you really like what you see. You then ask your dad if what the man sent was respectful and ask for his opinion. If the two of you have a match, then your dad gives the young man a green light. Your dad sends him a reply giving him permission to correspond and asks him always to treat you with courtesy and respect. Your dad may also offer to pray for your relationship.

If your dad gives you a red light, or even a caution light, about this man, follow his lead. This might be tough on you, but God may be warning you through your dad. God has given dads the chief responsibility to guard members of the family.

For example, it was to St. Joseph that God sent the angel to warn and to protect the Holy Family from King Herod. St. Joseph was the protector of his family in the first century, just as your dad is your family protector in the twenty-first century. If you don't have a father, then you can ask another family member to fulfill this role. In Bible times, the elder brother served in the father's absence. A good substitute for your father would be the man you would ask to walk you down the aisle when you're married.

By now I know what you might be thinking: "Who will ever e-mail me when they have to get my dad's permission!" First of all, I'll tell you who you'll hear very little from: immature boys, chat room predators, men looking for a cheap online thrill, and guys just looking for an interesting date to dump later. This "use your dad" strategy will keep online heartaches and headaches out of your life.

Second, I'll tell you who will write you. It will be the kind of man who loves a woman who presents challenges he has to face (see chapter 3). To be quite honest, if I were a young single man again and had to contact a young woman's father before courting, I'd be nervous as anything, but I'd value the developing relationship much more for having to contact the woman's father first.

Bottom line? Use dear old Dad along with new technology to make electronic courtship a success.

## CHAPTER NINETEEN

# S

# Scarcity of Good Men . . . and What You Can Do About It

Many single Christian women feel there's a scarcity of eligible Christian men. I believe that this feeling has a factual basis. Here's why.

## Absent male Christians

According to reports in *New Man Magazine,* men who attend church in the United States are outnumbered three-to-one by men who avoid church.[23] These reports also said that a full eighty-five percent of all these "unchurched" men in the United States were previously active in churches. These alarming trends have been developing for over a century and a half.[24] Many church leaders seem unaware that this crisis exists, or perhaps they're unwilling to confront a crisis of such magnitude.

Many brush off the "absent male Christian" phenomenon by saying, "Men are just not spiritually inclined." However, in American Judaism, Islam, and Eastern religions, male attendance is almost twice that of females, while in Eastern Orthodoxy, male and female attendance is about equal.[25] Therefore, we can't rely on the blanket statement that men are just not as spiritually inclined as women. Some other factors must be present in Western Christianity to cause the lack of participation.

One significant contributor to the "absent male Christian" crisis is that American churches have been consciously and unconsciously feminized by a number of influences.[26] You need to realize that most men would almost rather die than be absorbed by such a highly feminized and effeminate culture as is present in many of the North American churches.

To turn this situation around will take at least a generation, *after* the problem is recognized and acknowledged and dramatic action is taken to reverse it. So far, the process hasn't even begun. Furthermore, the increasing acceptance of homosexuality within churches will only confirm to men their worst suspicions and will keep even more men from active church life.

For these reasons, I wouldn't expect a return of absent male Christians to North American church life any time soon. It's a bitter irony that feminized Protestant and Catholic churches are hurting women at a critical level—namely, by diminishing the pool of marriageable Christian men who are active in their churches.

## Cohabitation drives men away from marriage

To compound this alarming situation, the skyrocketing levels of cohabitation among Christians (and non-Christians) is driving down the marriage rate. About fifty percent of all marriages are preceded by cohabitation. The subtitle of a recent study by David Popenoe and Barbara Dafoe Whitehead aptly summarizes the effects of cohabitation on marriage: *Sex Without Strings, Relationships Without Rings.*[27]

Cohabitation drives down the incentive to commit to marriage. Why this is true isn't hard to figure out. If women are willing to offer their bodies to men without asking for the commitment of marriage, then men will ask themselves, "Why not enjoy the pleasures of physical relations without all the obligations?"

The number of men willing to commit to marriage declines as the length of cohabitation increases. Since only one-sixth of cohabiting relationships last as long as three years, women are enduring cycles of hook-up and break-up—a discouraging emotional wasteland. No wonder the marriage rates of women are at their lowest level in over one hundred years.

As with the feminization of the churches, I'm not overly optimistic about a quick turn-around in cohabitation rates. When was the last time you heard a solid sermon against cohabitation? There are some very notable exceptions (for a good one visit our Web site at www.familylifecenter.net and click on "Courtship"), but for the most part the pulpit silence on cohabitation is deafening.

For that reason, I repeat my statement that Christian women today truly are facing an unprecedented scarcity of good eligible Christian men, and will probably continue to do so for at least the next generation.

## Things to do despite the scarcity of good men

What should a Christian woman eager to find a suitable Christian mate do?

The first thing is to avoid pity parties and dump-on-men sessions with friends. These feed discouragement and bitterness. Most of all, avoid the "woe is me I'll never find a husband" attitude. Such despairing activities will breed faithlessness and hopelessness in your heart. Finally, avoid radical-feminist agendas that pitch highly negative messages about men, marriage, and mate selection.

Following Christ gets interesting in tough situations. Christianity is the world's best religion for utterly hopeless situations. Remember that our Leader in whom we've placed our trust for eternal life was crucified, died, was buried in a tomb and then rose again.

If Christ could get through Holy Week to Easter Sunday, He can get you to the altar with a good man. You must learn to trust Him in this pilgrimage. Your experience of trusting Christ at this important stage in your life will deepen your relationship with Him.

The prophet Elijah lived in a time of widespread religious collapse. In discouragement and despair, he went to a cave and cried out to God that he was the only righteous man left in Israel. Listen to what St. Paul says about this incident:

> Do you not know what the Scripture says of Elijah, how he pleads with God against Israel? "Lord, they have killed Thy prophets, they have demolished Thy altars, and **I alone am left**, and they seek my life." **But what is God's reply to him? "I have kept for myself seven thousand men** who have not bowed the knee to Baal." **So too at the present time there is a remnant, chosen by grace** (Romans 11:2-5, emphasis added).

You may want to make a screen saver for your computer using these verses, because I believe there's a remnant of eligible good Christian men in North America.[28]

### There are still many good eligible men

Over the past six years, I've spoken all over North America to thousands of Catholic men eager to become better husbands and fathers. When I started this outreach, I was frequently met with stark unbelief when I mentioned that I wanted to gather men into conferences to strengthen marriages and family life. Initially, I had to beg in order to get the opportunities to gather these men at our conferences.

Yet the men came and continue to come. I'll never forget one group of men in Canada who drove their SUV sixteen hours each way over mountain ranges to get to a father's conference. I knew that there were good men who had it in them to become more effective fathers. There are still good men out there willing to make a commitment to their marriage and family life.

My first offer to speak at a national conference on some of the topics contained in this book was turned down by the organizers. They thought my ideas were too radical for most people to accept today. It was a *déjà vu* experience, such as starting St. Joseph's Covenant Keepers all over again. Yet there are thousands of good men and women ready and willing for a return to honorable courtship. They just need the challenge to do so.

While most of the men I've met in St. Joseph's Covenant Keepers are already married, I have every confidence that God has reserved at least seven thousand good single Christian men in North America who would make good husbands. Your only question is how to find one in the midst of scarcity. Here are some suggestions.

## 1. Get beyond the distance problem.

God may have seven thousand men, but I can't guarantee that one lives on your block. Be open to the idea that God might have a prospective husband for you who lives far away.

I recently read the story of a woman from Wyoming on a Christian singles Web site who restricted the men wishing to correspond with her to those living in her region of the country. One particularly persistent man living in an entirely different part of the country kept writing her. She asked why he kept writing her since he lived so far away.

He answered that if he won a cash prize on a millionaire show, he would gladly cross the country to claim his prize. He felt that a good wife would be more valuable than a million-dollar prize. Humbly taken aback, she changed her mind and invited this man to keep writing her. They are now married.

Remember that men love challenges. I have a friend who, with his father, desired to go on a special Canadian wilderness fishing trip. They crossed half a continent to get into the region of Canada where they wanted to go. They then hired a pontoon plane and flew to a very remote lake. They enthusiastically waved good-bye to the plane that left them for an entire week without electricity, running water, plumbing, central heat, phones, Internet connections, and ESPN. And they did all this for fish!

When a man is ready to get married, distance won't be an obstacle in courting. Yes, the distance between families can make practicing courtship principles a little more difficult, but the principles can be successfully adapted to various circumstances. Just tell your man the courtship principles you want to follow and he should be able to propose a good plan—in short order.

## 2. Keep your eyes open for men you already know.

The psalmist prayed, "Open my eyes, that I may behold wondrous things out of Thy law" (Psalm 119:18). Many of you have had the experience of reading a familiar passage of Scripture for years when one day a verse just leaps off the page at you with sudden relevance.

The same type of thing might happen with a man you've known for years without having any romantic notions about him. Since it wasn't yet time for you to court, God might have put a veil over the eyes of your heart. But then, when it's the proper time to start courting, you might suddenly discover in a new way this man you've known for so long.

Heather worked as the church secretary and Thom worked on the construction of the church school, so they saw each other daily. Before Heather developed an interest in Thom, her friend and co-worker thought that Thom was someone Heather should be interested in. Yet it took a year and a half for both Heather and Thom to realize that they should start a relationship to see whether they were meant for each other.

You never know which one God might bring you from far away or from close at hand.

### 3. Accept assistance from good matchmakers.

Families interested in adopting a child have found that letting their friends know of their serious desire to adopt can shorten the waiting period from years to months. In a similar way, your friends can be of tremendous assistance in finding you a prospective spouse, just as Heather's friend and co-worker did in the story above. Wise friends may spot good possibilities before you do. So you shouldn't be embarrassed to let your close friends know that you're ready to find a good spouse.

Watching the matchmaker in the movie *Fiddler on the Roof* may frighten you from ever letting someone play that role for you. Yet you should be open to suggestions from family members and close friends with good judgment.

I remember reading a story of a church-going couple who noticed a handsome young man who made a regular practice of attending a Holy Hour.[29] This couple happened to be friends with an attractive young woman who was having difficulty meeting a young man who took his faith as seriously as she did.

The couple encouraged their meeting. This young man and woman are now married.

### 4. Use the Internet.

I think the Internet will quickly replace singles' bars and church singles' groups as the prime meeting place for people looking for a mate. Singles' bars have their obvious limitations. Most church singles' groups also have limitations in that they try to reach too wide a spectrum of people with very diverse interests and needs. You might find the average church singles' group to have never-married twenty-year-olds grouped together with twice-married divorcees and in some cases with widows and widowers.

The Internet can quickly group you with people of similar age, background, and beliefs. The Internet also has an uncanny ability to bring people together with similar interests, and it makes it easier to fend off uninvited and unwelcome advances that you might encounter in singles' groups. Cyberspace is thus one of the most effective places to meet other Christian singles, especially if you live in a community with few men who share your faith.

Remember to follow all the precautions outlined in chapter 18. Your discernment must not be put on hold just because you use a Christian singles site. Some Christian singles sites are far better than others. Spend your time on the sites that have developed a solid reputation.

### 5.  Go where the like-minded men are.

If you want to catch a fish, you go where you think the most fish are. If you want to make a sales contact, you attend meetings with the greatest likelihood of finding potential clients. If you want to find a good husband, it makes sense to go to those locations and events where you know a group of good men is likely to be gathered.

One good place is a regional religious conference, especially those organized for singles committed to courtship.[30] Conferences such as these tend to draw committed believers from an entire geographic area.

Another excellent location for finding a good husband is at a Christian college. For those of you who can't afford the tuition of a private college, there's the low-budget option of getting a job on campus as a secretary or staff member. This will give you most of the advantages that any student has of meeting good Christian men.

### 6. Seize your moments of opportunity.

Your chances of finding a good husband are much greater if you're open to meeting someone while you're in your twenties than if you're in your thirties or forties. The reason is quite simple: there's a far larger pool of eligible men in the younger years.

Does this mean that your prospects for finding a good husband evaporate after age thirty? No, not at all. In fact, some young women might feel a call to serve God for several years as a single person before seeking a partner in marriage.

Some vital opportunites for service are much better fitted to a single person. If God is guiding you to postpone marriage, and yet you feel that He's also leading you to be married eventually, then my advice is to follow His lead and trust Him for the timely provision of a spouse. Consider as well whether God is actually calling you to the vocation of marriage or to another vocation (that is, the single or religious life).

I do think that you need to consider carefully whether you're putting secular career pursuits ahead of seeking a husband. The business world is increasingly opening up exciting and lucrative opportunities for women to achieve positions of prominence. So many talented women have put marriage on hold during their twenties and early thirties in order to achieve their career goals. Just when they should be brimming over with fulfillment from having achieved their goals, many of these women begin sensing a strange yearning for family life. After making themselves unavailable during their twenties and early thirties, they find that the pool of good eligible men has grown significantly smaller.

If you're in your teens or early twenties, then determine now what your life priorities are. If marriage is one of your priorities, you shouldn't allow a career to crowd out your best years for finding a husband.

# CHAPTER TWENTY

# T

## "To Have and To Hold . . ."

To have and to hold, for better, for worse, for richer, for poorer, in sickness and in health, from this day forward, until death do us part."

Wives like to be held in their husbands' arms. They like the confident embrace that reassures them that they will be held and treasured by their husbands throughout life. A marriage built upon an unconditional commitment of lifelong fidelity will give spouses the confidence to give of themselves unreservedly to each other. Lasting marital love requires the spousal commitment to be total, exclusive, and faithful.[31]

Nevertheless, our culture has eroded almost all of the traditional supports for lifelong marriage. It used to be that only Hollywood movie stars dissolved their marriages at whim. Now people from every segment of our entire society act this way, including Christians!

It used to be that when a middle-aged husband ran off with his twenty-something bleached-blonde secretary, we called him what he was: a despicable, dirty, rotten scoundrel. Today, we just shrug it off with the lame excuse that he's suffering from a mid-life crisis. In many states it's almost as easy to get a divorce as it is to get a driver's license. The astounding rates of divorce have eroded confidence in marriage, especially among young men and women. In response to this lowered trust in marriage, many couples are approaching it with timidity instead of certainty.

Contemporary couples often start out in marriage with a "let's try it and see if it works out" attitude. But these couples aren't ready for marriage. Nor are couples ready to wed who feel that they need a prenuptial agreement to serve as a legal parachute for their marriage.

Christian couples aren't prepared for marriage if they hold the poisonous attitude that says, "If our marriage doesn't work out, we can get a 'Christian divorce.'" Despite what you might read or hear on the airwaves, there's no such thing as a divorce from a valid Christian marriage, as Jesus made unmistakably clear in Mark 10:2-12.[32] And if a Catholic couple approaches the sacrament of marriage saying, "Let's give it a try; if it doesn't work out we can always get an annulment," then they're not ready for marriage, either.

The *Catechism*, describing the fidelity required for marriage, says this:

> Love seeks to be definitive; it cannot be an arrangement "until further notice." The "intimate union of marriage, as a mutual giving of two persons, and the good of the children, demand total fidelity from the spouses and require an unbreakable union between them." The deepest reason is found in the fidelity of God to His covenant, in that of Christ to his Church. . . .

It can seem difficult, even impossible, to bind oneself for life to another human being. This makes it all the more important to proclaim the Good News that God loves us with a definitive and irrevocable love, that married couples share in this love, that it supports and sustains them, and that by their own faithfulness they can be witnesses to God's faithful love.[33]

## The two "C" words: commitment and covenant

Many men and women today are scared of the word "commitment." In fact, some men go into complete panic when they hear the "C" word. Yet one-hundred percent commitment is required for a successful marriage. If you or a prospective spouse are not capable of making a total and complete commitment to each other, then you need to postpone marriage plans until you're ready to do so.

Successful marriages aren't built upon fifty/fifty commitments. That's only for civil contracts. Marriage covenants are made when spouses unreservedly give one hundred percent of themselves to each other.

In marriage, nothing is held in reserve. Nothing is excluded in the mutual giving of spouses to each other. This total and mutual self-giving is what joins the husband and wife, previously two separate individuals living two separate lives, into a new and mysterious oneness. The Bible says that they are no longer two, but one (see Genesis 2:24). There's nothing in all of human life quite like the mystery of marital oneness.

Because of its essential nature, the marriage covenant excludes everyone except one spouse. So long as the two of you are still alive, no one is allowed to take your place for any reason. Since marriage is a living icon of the faithful bond that Christ has for His Church, marital infidelity or divorce can never be considered as an option for a valid Christian marriage. That's why Christian couples are required to pledge solemn vows in the presence of God to have lifelong fidelity toward each other.

I compare the confidence needed in marriage to the confidence a sailor needs in the ship's anchor. Whenever I'm sleeping on a boat at anchor, I don't permit myself to get lost in a good night's sleep, even though I may be exhausted from a long day on the water. Throughout the night, I listen to the waves slapping against the side of the boat as an indication that the wind hasn't switched directions, making it easy for the anchor to lose its hold. Only when I have complete assurance of a secure mooring can I rest easy.

Similarly, marital love can't flourish in a climate of doubt. If you don't have assurance of total, exclusive, and faithful love, then you'll be plagued with nagging worries. Will he let go of me? Would he still love me if my health changed, or my facial appearance were instantly altered in an automobile accident? Will he abandon me in middle age for a younger plaything?

The pre-engagement period is the best time for close second and third evaluations. Even during the engagement period evaluations can be made. This book has probably encouraged more premarital consideration than most of the advice you've heard to date. Yet caution and hesitancy are appropriate *before* marriage. Once you're married, the time for second thoughts is over—forever. Married life is the time for reckless abandonment to unconditional love.

## CHAPTER TWENTY-ONE

# U

# Ultimate Marriage Buster

A study commissioned by the Marriage Project at Rutgers University found that eighty percent of young people say their number-one priority is a lasting marriage. Surely every marriage should begin with soaring hopes and expectations for a lifetime of love. Your wedding day should be the day when your dreams come true. So why are so many marital dreams turning into the nightmare of divorce?

Reasons abound for the multitude of marital breakups occurring all around us. I've tried to identify many of the reasons in this book so you can avoid them. Nevertheless, one particular contributor to divorce stands out above all others. This ultimate marriage buster is contraception, embraced by ninety-seven percent of young married couples even though it threatens the core of their marital relationship.

## Five-hundred percent increase in the divorce rate

The divorce rate has increased five hundred percent since the ultimate marriage buster started gaining popular acceptance early in the twentieth century. The ultimate marriage buster was given a big boost by medical technology in the 1960s, and the divorce rate has doubled since then. In fact, the divorce rate for new marriages hovers at fifty percent. In stark contrast, those married couples wise enough to keep the marriage buster out of their bedrooms have a divorce rate under five percent.[34]

Divorce has become a national concern. Government leaders, social agencies, university researchers, church leaders, and marital counselors are diligently searching for ways to improve marital stability. Individual Americans are spending more than a hundred million dollars every year on books, tapes, seminars, and therapy in an attempt to discover the secret glue that will hold contemporary marriages together. Strangely absent in our national search for marital stability is a public recognition and identification of the practice of artificial birth control as the ultimate buster of modern marriage.

Why does avoiding the ultimate marriage buster cause the probability of divorce to plummet from fifty percent to less than five percent? To answer this critical question, you must know something about the uniqueness of marital love between spouses.

## Marital love involves the innermost being of husband and wife

If asked, millions of Americans probably couldn't answer the question, "What's the difference between two animals copulating and a husband and wife expressing love in the marital embrace?" Yet the difference is deeply significant. While animal copulation is something purely biological, marital love is much, much more. Listen carefully to what the *Catechism* says:

> Sexuality, by means of which man and woman give
> themselves to one another through the acts which

are proper and exclusive to spouses, is not something simply biological, but concerns the innermost being of the human person as such. It is realized in a truly human way only if it is an integral part of the love by which a man and woman commit themselves totally to one another until death.[35]

## Total giving in marital love

Marital love is expressed in the total giving of oneself—body, mind, and heart—to one's spouse. This profound union goes beyond just the union of bodies. It's the complete union of persons joining the innermost cores of their being.

That's why the *Catechism* goes on to say that "conjugal love involves a totality, in which all the elements of the person enter—appeal of the body and instinct, power of feeling and affectivity, aspiration of the spirit and of will. It aims at a deeply personal unity, a unity that, beyond union in one flesh, leads to forming one heart and soul; it demands *indissolubility* and *faithfulness* in definitive mutual giving; and it is open to *fertility*."[36]

## The Berlin Wall between spouses

Artificial birth control erects a Berlin Wall between spouses, frustrating the intimate union of marriage. Artificial birth control speaks in silent language, "I give you some of myself, maybe even most of myself, but not all of myself." This partial giving creates a corrosive selfishness at the core of your marital union.

In contrast, genuine marital love, expressed in a sacred language of the body, says, "I give you myself—all of myself—without reservation." What happens when marital love is expressed in this total, self-giving manner? The *Catechism* describes it this way: "The acts in marriage by which the intimate and chaste union of the spouses takes place are noble and honorable; the truly human performance of these acts fosters the self-giving they signify and enriches the spouses in joy and gratitude."[37]

## Breaking commandments leads to broken marriages

By practicing artificial birth control, couples not only shut out their love for each other; they also damage their relationship with God. Breaking God's commands in marriage results in a multitude of broken marriages.

Since the first marriage in the Garden of Eden, God has commanded two purposes for marriage: *love making* (the unitive: "the two shall become one flesh," Genesis 2:24) and *life giving* (the procreative: "be fruitful and multiply," Genesis 1:28). Just as it is with the damage from cohabitation, when we engage in practices at odds with our Creator's design, things break. When we sever the bond of *love making* from *life giving*, marriages break—by the millions.

## The twofold purpose of marriage

The *Catechism* continues this original teaching on marriage:

> The spouses' union achieves the twofold end of marriage: the good of the spouses themselves and the transmission of life. These two meanings or values of marriage cannot be separated without altering the couple's spiritual life and compromising the goods of marriage and the future of the family.
>
> So the Church . . . teaches that "each and every marriage act must remain open to the transmission of life." "This particular doctrine, expounded on numerous occasions by the

Magisterium, is based on the inseparable con-
nection, established by God, which man on his
own initiative may not break, between the unitive significance and the procreative significance
which are both inherent to the marriage act."[38]

Christian morality thus forbids sterilization (vasectomies or tu-
bal ligations), contraceptive devices, and acts consciously intended to interrupt coitus and thwart procreation.

## An ecumenical morality—until recently

For nineteen out of the past twenty centuries, *all* Christian de-
nominations forbade these practices as gravely sinful. Most
modern readers are surprised to learn that *all* the major Protestant leaders such as Martin Luther, John Calvin, and John Wesley
taught that artificial contraception and unnatural acts to thwart
procreation destroyed the souls of those engaging in such practices.[39]

## Natural Family Planning

The sacredness of the marital union is not violated when couples
enjoy their embrace during infertile times. So if there are serious reasons to limit or space births, couples can morally practice what is called Natural Family Planning (NFP). When used
for proper reasons, Natural Family Planning doesn't violate the
twofold ends of marriage (*love making* and *life giving*).

The trustworthy teaching of the papal encyclical *Humanae Vitae*
[*Of Human Life*] says: "If, then, there are serious motives to space
out births . . . it is then licit to take into account the natural
rhythms immanent in the generative functions, for the use of
marriage in the infecund [infertile] periods only, and in this way
to regulate birth without offending the moral principles which
have been recalled earlier."[40]

A first-rate premarital training program should regard thorough training in Natural Family Planning as important as communication, compatibility, and family finances. Some premarital classes devote only a few minutes to Natural Family Planning; other classes completely ignore the topic. Both of these approaches are huge mistakes. Make certain that you have NFP training, even if you have to go outside your premarital classes to get it. NFP classes are taught throughout the country by competent couples.[41]

Christians during the twentieth century were foolish enough to imagine that abandoning God's design for marital love would bring liberation and happiness. In your selection of a husband, be certain that you have a solemn agreement with your fiancé to keep the ultimate marriage buster completely out of your marriage. You don't want to repeat the last century's mistakes.

## CHAPTER TWENTY-TWO

# V

# Vocation of Marriage

Most of us hear the word *vocation* and think of a career, a profession, an occupation, or a trade. The word comes from a Latin root meaning *to call.* The Catholic teaching on vocation is that God personally calls us to a particular path He has laid out for us to follow in life. This divine call involves far more than an occupational decision. It's a call from God to a particular state of life: the vocations of marriage, the priesthood, consecrated life in a religious order, single life, or the permanent diaconate.[42]

## Focus on your vocation

The Catholic understanding of the vocation of marriage is particularly helpful in our culture, which tends to assume that your work defines who you are and that the level of your salary determines your personal worth. The Church teaches us, on the contrary, that while our jobs are important, they should never eclipse the importance of the vocation to marriage.

Our culture is ready to lead the married into an all-consuming spousal relationship with their careers. The resulting misplaced priorities invariably damage marriage and family life. When the regrets finally surface, it's often too late to make up for the lost time. If God is calling you to the vocation of marriage, then you must stay focused on your vocation.

Once you determine God's vocation for your life, you can select a career path that will enable you to fulfill your vocation. For instance, if God is calling you to be a wife and mother, then it might be wise to learn skills that would permit you to work in a home-based business.

Many women have spent the prime years for finding a good mate and starting a family in an all-consuming climb up the corporate ladder. Only too late do they discover that such a path has led them away from their vocation. I'm not suggesting that women shouldn't devote themselves to the corporate life; I only recommend determining your vocation *before* embarking on a career path.

## The need for quiet time in an age of noise

In order to hear your personal call, you need to give God some quiet time. I'll suggest something really radical. I recommend that you unplug your stereo for at least an hour every day and enjoy some quiet time.

Novelist Michael O'Brien has accurately described our times as an "age of noise."[43] Everywhere we go, all day long and well into the night, our electronic gadgets give us non-stop noise. So each of us needs to make some quiet time for meditation each day.

Mornings are the best time to listen to the gentle nudging of the Holy Spirit (see Psalm 119:147; Wisdom 16:28; Sirach 32:14, 39:5). With a listening heart read Scripture, pray, and just sit in silence. A quiet morning or evening walk is also a good way to maintain an open ear. Before making a major decision, I find a quiet hour in the sanctuary in the presence of the Blessed Sacrament to be indispensable for determining God's direction for me.

Whatever vocation God calls you to, it will be the path on which you'll find deep joy and satisfaction of heart. If He's calling you to marriage, then joyfully follow Him on the path to holiness in married life. This call is twofold: first to marriage, and second to a specific person. Pray that God's will can be revealed so that you'll recognize the person He intends for you.

## CHAPTER TWENTY-THREE

# W

# Wine—a Blessing and a Marriage Buster

One of my most enjoyable times after a long workweek is "date night" with my wife at one of our favorite restaurants, slowly sipping wine together. It's hard to imagine life getting better than this pleasant and relaxing way to share married life. Surely God is good in giving "wine to gladden the heart of man" (Psalm 104:15).

Nevertheless, my wife and I are willing to suspend our enjoyment of wine whenever we realize that someone joining us for dinner abstains because they have an alcoholic family background or because they have personal struggles with alcoholism. Christian charity requires that we abstain if our actions could become a cause of stumbling. St. Paul says, "It is right not to eat meat or drink wine or do anything that makes your brother stumble. We who are strong ought to bear with the failings of the weak, and not to please ourselves" (Romans 14:21, 15:1).

For twenty-five years in ministry, I've seen alcoholism's pernicious ability to mangle marriages and fracture families. Over and again, I've observed that it's a small step from merrymaking with wine to marital melancholy due to alcoholism. So if I thought either of us had crossed the threshold into the early stages of alcoholism, I'd abstain permanently. My marriage means infinitely more to me than a half carafe of wine!

## Warnings about alcohol abuse

The Bible says that wine is a blessing from God. It was used in the Old Testament for sacrifices and rejoicing on feast days. Jesus performed His first miracle by turning water into wine at the wedding of Cana. St. Paul even said that wine mixed with water has medicinal value (1 Timothy 5:23).

Yet in contrast to all these positive biblical statements about alcohol, we also read a host of warnings about the dangers associated with too much of a good thing. Here's a sampling of the many biblical warnings and exhortations about drunkenness:

> "Let us conduct ourselves becomingly as in the day, not in reveling and drunkenness" (Romans 13:13).

> "Now the works of the flesh are plain . . . envy, drunkenness, carousing, and the like. I warn you, as I warned you before, that those who do such things shall not inherit the kingdom of God" (Galatians 5:19-21).

> "And do not get drunk with wine, for that is debauchery; but be filled with the Spirit" (Ephesians 5:18).

> "Let the time that is past suffice for doing what the Gentiles like to do, living in licentiousness, passions, drunkenness, revels, carousing, and lawless idolatry" (1 Peter 4:3).

"Woe to those who are heroes at drinking wine, and valiant men in mixing strong drink" (Isaiah 5:22).

"Wine is a mocker, strong drink a brawler; and whoever is led astray by it is not wise" (Proverbs 20:1).

"Who has woe? Who has sorrow? Who has strife? Who has complaining? Who has wounds without cause? Who has redness of eyes? Those who tarry long over wine, those who go to try mixed wine. Do not look at wine when it is red, when it sparkles in the cup and goes down smoothly. At the last it bites like a serpent, and stings like an adder. Your eyes will see strange things, and your mind utter perverse things" (Proverbs 23:29-33).

## Turning men into beasts and barbarians

Too much wine and whiskey can turn gentlemen into beasts and barbarians, bringing out the very worst in them. I thought that I'd seen a lot of drunken fighting in high school and on a major university campus. But that was nothing compared to what I saw sailors do when I was stationed in Guantanamo Bay, Cuba.

Being on an island military base surrounded by Communist troops, we didn't have much to do at night except drink. Kegs of cheap beer and hard liquor were consumed for hours on weeknights and on weekends at servicemen's clubs. Practically every night on the way back to their ships and barracks the Marines and Navy servicemen would provoke brutal fights with each other. Drunkenness made comrades nearly dismember each other. And unfortunately for families, such drunken aggression is not limited to military bases.

Too much alcohol can cause men to say and to do things to their families that they'll later deeply regret. Ask any law enforcement officer about the main ingredient in the endless cases of domestic abuse, and he'll tell you that booze leads to bruises. The first recorded instances of incest in the Bible followed drunkenness (see Genesis 19:30-36). Alcohol destroys millions of marriages every year, while leaving a legacy of scarred hearts in the children of alcoholics.

In addition, thousands of unmarried men and women have succumbed to sexual temptation because they had too much to drink while on a date. You'd be wise to keep all your senses about you while courting.

## A letter that can prevent a lifetime of misery

The wisest commentary I've ever read on alcoholism is a two-page letter from Dr. Anderson Spickard, professor of medicine at the Vanderbilt Medical Center and director of the Vanderbilt Center for the Treatment of Alcoholism. Through his research and experience, Dr. Spickard has determined that *the majority of our nation's ten million alcoholics come from families with an inherited tendency.*[44]

One special study highlighting the genetic predisposition for alcoholism focused on men who had alcoholic fathers but were adopted at birth by other families. Even without the environmental influence of being raised by their alcoholic fathers, these men were found to be nine times as likely to develop an addiction as children of non-alcoholic fathers.[45] Dr. Spickard warns that alcoholism travels down family lines to such a degree that sixty to eighty percent of alcoholics have parents, grandparents, siblings, aunts or uncles who are also alcoholics.

117

Dr. Spickard writes his two-page letter to the children and grand-children of the alcoholics he treats. He warns them of the genetic disposition for alcoholism and suggests total abstinence as the wisest preventative. You too should heed his warning: there's great wisdom in abstaining if either you or your future spouse have a family history of alcoholism.

Many women fall for the charms of an outgoing guy who's the life of every party. Only too late do they realize they've married an alcoholic who deprives their marriage of happiness and warps their home into a living hell. If you're courting a man who's a hero at drinking, then I'd suggest you attend a couple of Alcoholics Anonymous meetings to sober up your marital decision-making process.

Wine in moderation is a blessing from God to gladden hearts. Yet alcohol taken to excess is heartbreaking. *Temperance* is not a dirty word. It's the virtue that, according to the *Catechism,* "moderates the attraction of pleasures and provides balance in the use of created goods. It ensures the will's mastery over instincts and keeps desires within the limits of what is honorable."[46] Make sure that the man you marry is a temperate man.

## CHAPTER TWENTY-FOUR

# X

# X-ray His Words and His Heart

If you want to know what's in a man's heart, then listen attentively to him. Wisdom from the book of Sirach says, "If you love to listen you will gain knowledge, and if you incline your ear you will become wise" (6:33).

## Active listening

In premarital and marital counseling, I've found that careful listening is the most important skill I have to offer a couple. Truly attentive listening is work and requires concentration, but it always rewards the listener with knowledge of the other person. Speech is the window into the heart. Jesus said, "The tree is known by its fruit . . . For out of the abundance of the heart the mouth speaks. The good man out of his good treasure brings forth good, and the evil man out of his evil treasure brings forth evil" (Matthew 12:33-35).

## Good men use pure speech

The type of man you're interested in uses pure speech; is hesitant to gossip; speaks kindly of others, even those he disagrees with; uses his tongue with kindness to build others up; and always speaks respectfully to his parents and family members.

## The consequences of marrying a man with an unruly tongue

The type of man you want to avoid uses profanity, even in the presence of women; is quick to give others a tongue-lashing; tells vulgar jokes; and is frequently critical of others. Be warned that if you marry a man with an angry tongue, his anger will be directed at you in marriage. If a man is sharply critical of others, then you will most certainly find him harshly critical of you. If you hear him verbally tear down others, then his tongue will be slashing at his wife. If his tongue utters profane words, then his heart is filled with things you don't want to join your heart to.

Wisdom from the book of Proverbs says, "A gentle tongue is a tree of life, but perverseness in it breaks the spirit. Death and life are in the power of the tongue" (15:4, 18:21). A husband's harsh tongue can be like a pile driver crushing the spirit of his wife. In contrast, a good husband's tongue refreshes the spirit of his wife. So X-ray the heart of any man you become interested in by carefully listening to him. What you hear is a good predictor of what will come out of his mouth in marriage.

## CHAPTER TWENTY-FIVE

# Y

# Your Knight in Shining Armor

B y this point in the book you're probably asking yourself, "How will I ever meet a man who meets all these standards?" There are thousands of good men who have the potential to be suitable courtiers, who just need a nudge in the right direction. I believe that the impulse to re-establish the practice of courtship in this new millennium will come from women of high standards, character, civility, charm, modesty, and chastity.

It's easy to get discouraged thinking that most of the guys you've encountered are light-years from the standards for courtship in these pages. But don't just look at the legion of immature nineteen-year-olds, whose highest skill is consumerism, whose ambition in life is vegetating on others' money, whose relational skills are mired in self-absorption. Without a significant challenge, men like these revel in immaturity.

Instead, think of how the U.S. Army can transform nineteen-year-olds into the type of soldier who will storm Omaha Beach on D-Day. Yes, there are hordes of twenty-year-olds who can't get themselves out of bed in the morning, but the Navy can train a twenty-year-old to hold the responsibility of piloting a two-billion-dollar submarine. The military has a vision of what men can be, and they succeed in making men out of undisciplined youth.

## Men today are capable of gallantry

Always remember that men are capable of great gallantry. Christians often underestimate men's potential. The organization called Promise Keepers absolutely amazed thousands of pastors (and wives) who never dreamed that so many men would respond to a challenge to be men of integrity. When I began St. Joseph's Covenant Keepers, many people I spoke with couldn't imagine that young Catholic men would respond to a firm challenge to raise their standards in their marriage and family life.

What has been the result? I've personally seen thousands of men respond to the high calling of following Jesus. Men have written us from over forty foreign countries wanting to know more about the challenge of St. Joseph's Covenant Keepers. Will younger single men respond to a similar challenge? I think a legion of young men eagerly waits to respond to the call of courtship.

## The need for challenging men to gallantry

How will this call come to young men? I see it coming from two directions. First, I see organizations such as St. Joseph's Covenant Keepers and many other fine Christian men's organizations directing challenges toward young men. I foresee father-son conferences where these themes are presented so fathers can help inspire their sons to greatness in courtship.

The second source calling young men to courtship will blossom from the quiet convictions of young Christian women. How will this occur? On the simplest level, I expect that many men will secretly read this book once they find out that some attractive Christian women are following its advice. Word will spread among the guys, and many of them will truly want to become the type of men these women are looking for.

As author George Gilder has argued, women are the civilizing agents for men in society.[47] Men without good women become barbarians fixated on self-destructive behavior. But with good wives, they become gallant at self-sacrificing for the welfare of their families and communities.

In many ways, women set the level that men rise to in courtship and marriage. Will single Christian women lose hope and lower the bar in their expectations for a spouse, or will they raise the standard and play a vital role in creating modern knights? To a significant degree, the future of single men lies in the hands of women just like you. Which path will you take?

Courtship may be a grossly outdated word for many, but let me tell you what courtship will do for some fine men who encounter modern versions of it.

## Courtship and knighthood

The word pictures suggested by courtship go back to the royal court where a young knight or prince would woo a maiden. Courtship is associated with the chivalry and honor of knighthood. Words such as courage, character, honor, gallantry, sacrifice, courtesy (a court-like politeness), magnanimity, virtue, integrity, fidelity are not just nice expressions. They're calls to action that can inspire a man to greatness. A knight knew who he was and what he stood for.

There are two paths for modern mate selection. Along one path lie the flimsy and seldom-lasting relationships in which young men and women treat each other merely as objects for personal pleasure and fulfillment. On the higher path, you'll find men of gallantry seeking a soul mate to share lifelong love in the sacrament of marriage.

## Who said dreams can't come true?

You've dreamed of that special knight who will appear and claim you for his own forever. Don't let your dreams dissipate. Men of character and virtue are still out there. One is waiting just for you.

Where do you think that deep desire for a really good man came from? Of course, it's your Creator who puts such desires in women's hearts. If He put such a desire in your heart, don't you believe that He's capable of fulfilling it?

> "Take delight in the LORD, and He will give you the desires of your heart" (Psalm 37:4).

## CHAPTER TWENTY-SIX

# Z

# Zero in on What I'm Saying

The first person to read the manuscript of this book was a woman, a divorcee, whom I'll call Janelle. Janelle called me because she was seriously interested in any information that could help her avoid repeating the painful experiences of her first marriage. She knows firsthand how deep and lasting are the wounds from a broken marriage. Janelle is eager to learn how to avoid mistakes in mate selection.

Many of you reading this book come from broken homes. As an adult child of divorce, you know the pain and are eager to learn how to prevent marriage breakup by starting your courtship off on the right foot. Like Janelle, you're highly motivated to implement what you've learned from reading *The ABCs of Choosing a Good Husband*.

Many of us have to learn life's lessons the hard way before we become open to listening to wisdom. If you fit into this category, be warned: there's a huge difference between life lessons about marriage and life lessons about other experiences. Unlike many other mistakes in life, marriage mistakes have consequences that are internal and lifelong.

Marriage permanently bonds you—heart, soul, and body—to another person. If you make a big mistake in selecting a marriage partner, then the "oneness" of marriage cannot be completely undone. Even if you get a divorce and move a thousand miles from your estranged spouse, a part of you will always be with him, and a part of him will always be with you. In the deepest part of your heart, the pain will be with you. If a divorce occurs with children, then this pain will travel on to the next generation.

Therefore, I urge you: after reading this book, put into action all that you've learned. The steps you take now while on the road toward marriage will have lasting effects for better or for worse. Only reading and talking about the *ABCs* will have zero beneficial effect. If you want to succeed in your marriage, then you must translate them into practice.

I want your marriage to be a foretaste of heaven on earth. I want you to enjoy the blessings of a long, happy marriage. As I said in the introduction, by following and by doing *all* the *ABCs*, you should experience a seventy-five percent reduction in the probability of suffering a divorce.

Right now, that seventy-five percent figure is just an educated guess. I'd like to hear from you if you decide to go the entire distance and make the *ABCs* your blueprint for selection of a marriage partner. Please contact us again when you get married and let us know your address. With you and your husband's permission, we'd like to follow up on the success of your marriage. Your story, coupled with others like yours, will help others learn to write their own stories of lasting love.

There comes a time in a courting relationship to take the step of faith. Throughout this book, I've advocated caution and deliberative decision making in choosing a spouse. But once you and your prospective mate have followed the steps recommended in this book and are certain that you're meant for each other, don't let fear paralyze you from taking the final step and committing to marriage.

## Don't be afraid of marriage

Risk is unavoidable if you want to achieve anything great. There's risk involved in entrusting your love to another in the sacrament of marriage. But as Pope John Paul II has repeated throughout his pontificate, and especially on the eve of crossing the threshold into a new millennium, "Be not afraid!"

You should enjoy the abiding certainty that God is with you in the entire mate-selection process. Don't be afraid. If God has called you to the vocation of marriage, then at the right time He'll bring a good man into your life. Do your part in the responsible choosing of a husband, but also be aware that in every step of the process you and your future husband are being upheld by God's hand.

St. Peter is sometimes overly criticized for his impetuous nature. When the disciples saw Jesus walking on the water they were all terrified and cried out in fear. Yet only St. Peter had the faith to leave the security of the boat and walk to Jesus on the water. Fear and hesitancy kept all the others in the boat. Sure, St. Peter had his moment of doubt while walking on the water, but he cried out for the Savior's help. And according to St. Matthew, "Jesus immediately reached out his hand and caught him" (14:31).

If God has called you to marriage and provided a good man for you to marry, don't let fear keep you from venturing on the path leading through courtship to marriage. Marriage is one of life's greatest blessings, and it's well worth the venture. If things get a little unsteady on your journey toward the altar, just ask for the Good Shepherd's hand to steady your steps. He's always with you on your way.

May God grant you a godly, handsome, and loving husband, along with many happy years of married life.

# Appendix

## Timeless Advice on Choosing a Marriage Partner by Pope Pius XI

To the proximate preparation of a good married life belongs very specially the care in choosing a partner; on that depends a great deal whether the forthcoming marriage will be happy or not, since one may be to the other either a great help in leading a Christian life, or a great danger and hindrance. And so that they may not deplore for the rest of their lives the sorrows arising from an indiscreet marriage, those about to enter into wedlock should carefully deliberate in choosing the person with whom henceforward they must live continually: they should, in so deliberating, keep before their minds the thought first of God and of the true religion of Christ, then of themselves, of their partner, of the children to come, as also of human and civil society, for which wedlock is a fountainhead.

Let them diligently pray for divine help, so that they make their choice in accordance with Christian prudence, not indeed led by the blind and unrestrained impulse of lust, nor by any desire of riches or other base influence, but by a true and noble love and by a sincere affection for the future partner; and then let them strive in their married life for those ends for which the State was constituted by God.

Lastly, let them not omit to ask the prudent advice of their parents with regard to the partner, and let them regard this advice in no light manner, in order that, by their mature knowledge and experience of human affairs, they may guard against a disastrous choice, and, on the threshold of matrimony, may receive more abundantly the divine blessing of the fourth commandment: "Honor thy father and thy mother (which is the first commandment with a promise) that it may be well with thee and thou mayest be long-lived upon the earth."[48]

# Endnotes

1   Adapted with permission from *Dynamic Preaching*, May 1989, Christian
    Communications Laboratory, P.O. Box 10965, Knoxville, TN 37939.

2   The St. Michael's Institute (online go to www.saintmichael.net) is a
    national alliance of mental health professionals who integrate the
    genuine discoveries of psychology and psychiatry with the teaching of
    the Catholic Church. This organization is a good place to start in
    locating a counselor. The Institute for the Psychological Sciences in
    Arlington, Va. (phone: 703-416-1441; Web site: www.cips-usa.org) is
    training a new generation of psychologists who also integrate their
    scientific and therapeutic careers with Christian faith. Talking with
    graduates from this Institute is another good starting place in your
    search for a good counselor.

    Because we're not personally familiar with every person affiliated with
    or recommended by these two institutes, we cannot guarantee that a
    particular counselor they might recommend is reliable. You need to
    consult local clergy, mental health experts, and other nearby competent
    professionals before acting upon any referral. Make sure that any
    counselor you select is committed to keeping marriages together. Many
    counselors claim to be "neutral" on the issue of divorce, believing that
    individual fulfillment is more important than maintaining the marriage
    relationship.

3   See Beth L. Bailey, *From Front Porch to Back Seat: Courtship in
    Twentieth-Century America* (Baltimore: Johns Hopkins University Press,
    1988).

4   Michael J. McManus, *Marriage Savers: Helping Your Friends and
    Family Stay Married* (Grand Rapids, Mich.: Zondervan, 1993), pp. 134-
    136. See also online: www.marriagesavers.org.

5   "Values Will Matter at Patrick Henry," *The Washington Times Weekly
    Edition*, July 31, 2000, reporting on Patrick Henry College in Falls
    Church, Va.

[6] David Popenoe and Barbara Dafoe Whitehead, *Should We Live To-gether? What Young Adults Need to Know About Cohabitation Before Marriage* (Brunswick, N.J.: The National Marriage Project, 1999), p. 2. See also online: http://marriage.rutgers.edu/publicat.htm.

[7] David Popenoe and Barbara Dafoe Whitehead, *Sex Without Strings, Relationships Without Rings: Today's Young Singles Talk About Mating and Dating* (Brunswick, NJ: The National Marriage Project, 2000), p. 7. See also online: http://marriage.rutgers.edu/publicat.htm.

[8] For an extensive list of problems associated with cohabiting, visit the "All About Cohabiting Before Marriage" Web site at http://hometown.aol.com/cohabiting/index.htm.

[9] Barbara Dafoe Whitehead, "How We Mate," *City Journal*, Summer 1999, p. 4. See also online: www.city-journal.org/.

[10] Whitehead, "How We Mate," p. 6.

[11] McManus, p. 91.

[12] *Family in America Report* (The Rockford Institute, 934 North Main Street, Rockford, Ill., 61103), February 1996, p. 2-3, reporting on a study by Jessie M. Tzeng of McGill University and Robert D. Mare of the University of Wisconsin-Madison, who interviewed 12,686 men and women, with annual follow-up interviews for eight years.

[13] *Family in America Report*, February 1996, pp. 2-3.

[14] *Catechism of the Catholic Church*, par. 1652, quoting *Gaudium et Spes*, 48.

[15] David H. Olson, John Defrain, and Amy K. Olson, *Building Relationships: Developing Skills for Life* (Minneapolis, MN: Life Innovations, 1999), pp. 89-90. The chart of couple satisfaction is reproduced with the permission of David Olson.

[16] Olson *et al.*, pp. 89-90.

[17] Joshua Harris, *I Kissed Dating Goodbye* (Sisters, Ore.: Multnomah, 1997) and *Boy Meets Girl: Say Hello to Courtship* (Sisters, Ore: Multnomah, 2000).

[18] *Catechism*, par. 234.

[19] Quoted in the *Catechism*, par. 2365.

[20] James Burnham and Stephen Wood, *Christian Fatherhood: The Eight Commitments of St. Joseph's Covenant Keepers* (Port Charlotte, Fla.: Family Life Center Publications, 1997), pp. 153-154.

21 Pope Pius XI, *Christian Marriage* [*Casti Connubii*], par. 41, 43, 111.

22 A letter written in 1808 quoted in Ellen K. Rothman, *Hands and Hearts: A History of Courtship in America* (New York, Basic Books), p. 18.

23 George Barna, "The Battle for the Hearts of Men," *New Man Magazine*, January 1997, pp. 40-43, reporting results from a survey by the Barna Research Group.

24 Leon Podles, *The Church Impotent: The Feminization of Christianity* (Dallas: Spence Publishing Company, 1999), pp. ix-26, 154-163. While I do not agree with all his conclusions, Podles traces some of these feminization trends all the way back to the Middle Ages. Also, see my article, "The Double-Fisted Gospel: A Remedy for Absent Male Catholics," *St. Joseph's Covenant Keepers Newsletter,* Vol. 5, Issue 3, May-June 1999, pp.1-6. Available online at www.dads.org.

25 Podles, pp. ix, xii, 26, 28.

26 Podles, pp. 3-36, 196-198.

27 See note 7 above.

28 I confine my remarks to North America because that is where I have firsthand experience, but I believe that there are thousands of good men in all countries.

29 A Holy Hour is a Catholic devotional practice in the presence of the Blessed Sacrament that involves praying and reading Scripture for one hour based upon Christ's challenge in Matthew 26:40 and Mark 14:37 to "watch one hour."

30 The Family Life Center hopes to organize courtship conferences in the near future. Visit www.familylifecenter.net to see the latest conference schedule.

31 Cardinal Alfonso Lopez Trujillo, *Preparation for the Sacrament of Marriage* (Vatican City: Pontifical Council for the Family, 1996), par. 35. This document mentions a fourth aspect to marital love: namely, that it is *fruitful*. For this fourth characteristic, see chapter 7.

32 For a concise summary of the scriptural teachings on divorce and remarriage, see Burnham and Wood, *Christian Fatherhood*, pp. 147-154.

33 *Catechism,* par. 1646-1648.

[34] Janet E. Smith, *Humanae Vitae: A Generation Later* (Washington, D.C.: Catholic University of America Press, 1991), pp. 127, 391. Among spouses teaching Natural Family Planning with the Couple to Couple League, the divorce rate is 1.4 percent. It is estimated that the divorce rate for all couples using Natural Family Planning may be up to three times this number, or 4.2 percent, which is still less than a tenth of the national divorce rate.

[35] *Catechism*, par. 2361, quoting *Familiaris Consortio*, par. 11.

[36] *Catechism*, par. 1643, quoting *Familiaris*, par. 13.

[37] *Catechism*, par. 2362, quoting *Gaudium et Spes*, 49, 2.

[38] *Catechism*, par. 2363 and 2366, quoting *Humanae Vitae*, par. 11-12.

[39] Charles D. Provan, *The Bible and Birth Control* (Monongahela, Pa: Zimmer Printing, 1989), pp. 69-92.

[40] *Humanae Vitae*, par. 16.

[41] Contact the Couple to Couple League (www.ccli.org) headquartered in Cinncinnati, Ohio, for Natural Family Planning classes near you. Also, the Family Life Office in your Catholic diocese will be able to refer you to a NFP class.

[42] For an excellent handbook to use in discovering both your vocation and career, see Rick Sarkisian, *LifeWork: Finding Your Purpose in Life* (San Francisco: Ignatius Press, 1997).

[43] Michael D. O'Brien, *A Landscape with Dragons: The Battle for Your Child's Mind* (San Francisco: Ignatius Press, 1998), p. 164.

[44] Anderson Spickard, M.D., and Barbara R. Thompson, *Dying for a Drink: What You Should Know About Alcoholism* (Waco, Texas: Word, 1985), 194-195. Unfortunately, this excellent book is out of print. With Dr. Spickard's permission, we have posted his two-page letter at www.familylifecenter.net.

[45] Spickard, p. 194.

[46] See the *Catechism*, par. 1809.

[47] George Gilder, *Men and Marriage* (Gretna, La.: Pelican Publishing Company, 1992).

[48] *On Christian Marriage,* par. 115. Available for free download at www.familylifecenter.net.

# Bibliography

## Helpful Catholic resources

Carol, Angela. *St. Raphael.* Rockford, Illinois: TAN, 1999.

*Catechism of the Catholic Church.* Ligouri, Missouri: Ligouri, 1994. See especially par. 1601, 1666, 2331-2400.

Doyle, Charles Hugo. *Blame No One But Yourself: Marriage Counsels to Teen-Agers and All Those Contemplating Wedlock.* Tarrytown, New York: Nugent, 1955.

Elliott, Msgr. Peter. *What God Has Joined: The Sacramentality of Marriage.* New York: Alba House, 1990.

Healy, Edwin F., S.J. *Teacher's Manual for Marriage Guidance.* Chicago: Loyola University, 1949.

Kippley, John. *Marriage Is for Keeps: Foundations for Christian Marriage.* Cincinnati: Foundation for the Family, 1994.

Marks, Frederick W. *A Catholic Handbook for Engaged and Newly Married Couples.* Milford, Ohio: The Riehle Foundation, 1994.

National Conference of Catholic Bishops, Committee for Pastoral Research and Practices. *Faithful to Each Other Forever: A Catholic Handbook of Pastoral Help for Marriage Preparation.* Washington, DC: United States Catholic Conference, Office of Publishing and Promotion Services, 1989.

O'Brien, Rev. John A. *Courtship and Marriage: Happiness in the Home.* Patterson, NJ: St. Anthony Guild, 1949.

Sheen, Fulton J. *Three to Get Married.* Princeton: Scepter, 1951.

Trujillo, Cardinal Alfonso Lopez. *Preparation for the Sacrament of Marriage*. Vatican City: Pontifical Council for the Family, 1996.

von Hildebrand, Dietrich. *Marriage: The Mystery of Faithful Love*. Manchester, New Hampshire: Sophia Institute, 1991.

## Papal encyclicals on marriage and family life

(All papal encyclicals listed are available for free download from www.dads.org and www.familylifecenter.net.)

* Leo XIII, *On Christian Marriage* [*Arcanum Divinae*], 1880.

* Pius XI, *On Christian Marriage* [*Casti Connubii*], 1930.

* Paul VI, *Of Human Life* [*Humanae Vitae*], 1968.

* John Paul II, *The Role of the Christian Family in the Modern World* [*Familiaris Consortio*], 1981.

* John Paul II, *Letter to Families*, 1994.

## Other helpful resources

Bailey, Beth L. *From Front Porch to Back Seat: Courtship in Twentieth-Century America*. Baltimore: Johns Hopkins University, 1988.

Blankenhorn, David. *Fatherless America*. New York: Basic, 1995.

Dufoyer, Pierre. *Marriage: A Word to Young Men*. New York: P. J. Kennedy & Sons, 1963.

Eberly, Don E., ed. *The Faith Factor in Fatherhood*. Lanham, Maryland: Lexington, 1999.

Gallagher, Maggie. *Enemies of Eros: How the Sexual Revolution Is Killing Family, Marriage, and Sex and What We Can Do About It*. Chicago: Bonus, 1989.

Gottman, John. *Why Marriages Succeed or Fail . . . And How You Can Make Yours Last*. New York: Simon & Schuster, 1994.

Harris, Joshua. *I Kissed Dating Goodbye*. Sisters, Oregon: Multnomah, 1997.

Horn, Wade F., David Blankenhorn, and Mitchell B. Pearlstein, eds. *The Fatherhood Movement: A Call to Action*. Lanham, Maryland: Lexington, 1999.

Kass, Amy A. and Leon R. Kass, eds. *Wing to Wing, Oar to Oar: Readings on Courtship and Marrying*. Notre Dame, Indiana: University of Notre Dame, 2000.

Mason, Mike. *The Mystery of Marriage: As Iron Sharpens Iron*. Portland, Oregon: Multnomah, 1985.

McManus, Michael J. *Marriage Savers: Helping Your Friends and Family Avoid Divorce*. Grand Rapids: Zondervan, 1995.

Olson, David H., John DeFrain, and Amy K. Olson. *Building Relationships: Developing Skills for Life*. Minneapolis: Life Innovations, 1999.

Popenoe, David, and Barbara Dafoe Whitehead. *The State of Our Unions 2000: The Social Health of Marriage in America*. The National Marriage Project, Rutgers University, New Brunswick, New Jersey: June 2000. http://marriage.rutgers.edu/publicat.htm.

Popenoe, David, and Barbara Dafoe Whitehead. "Should We Live Together? What Young Adults Need to Know About Cohabitation Before Marriage." The National Marriage Project, Rutgers University, New Brunswick, New Jersey: Jan. 1999. http://marriage.rutgers.edu/publicat.htm.

Rothman, Ellen K. *Hands and Hearts: A History of Courtship in America*. New York: Basic Books, 1984.

Sollee, Diane. *Coalition for Marriage, Family, and Couples Education (CMFCE)*. An abundant collection of articles and resources for marriage and family life are posted on this helpful Web site. http://www.smartmarriages.com.

Voth, Harold M. *Families: The Future of America*. Chicago: Regnery Gateway, 1984.

Wright, H. Norman. *Premarital Counseling*. Chicago: Moody, 1977.

# Resources

**For any of the resources below
visit www.familylifecenter.net
or call 1-800-705-6131**

## Catalog

The Family Life Center offers a free catalog of a wide selection of tapes, books, and videos on courtship, marriage, faith, family life, and fatherhood. You can also order any items from our online catalog at www.familylifecenter.net.

## Conferences

The Family Life Center holds conferences throughout North America. For a list of upcoming conferences, visit our Web sites (www.familylifecenter.net and www.dads.org). The Family Life Center sponsors and participates in conferences on courtship, marriage, parenting, faith, and family life. To bring a speaker to your community, visit our website conference page to view available speakers along with their topics and fees. Request an information package for the speaker you are interested in by calling us or by sending us an email.

## Live Author Interviews

A six audio tape/CD set of live author interviews on *The ABCs of Choosing a Good Husband* is a perfect accompaniment to the book. These live interviews give you in-depth explanations and helpful tips related to the *ABCs*.

## Stuff for Men You Know

- *The ABCs of Choosing a Good Wife*, the companion *ABCs* book for guys.

- www.dads.org is a Web site for Christian husbands and fathers.

- Dads.org Newsletter, a free e-newsletter. Subscribe at www.dads.org.

- *Christian Fatherhood: The Eight Commitments of St. Joseph's Covenant Keepers* by Stephen Wood and James Burnham. A great book for any dad *and* for any young man preparing to be a husband and father.

### Extra copies

To order extra copies of either of the ABCs books for your friends and family members, call our toll-free number, 1-800-705-6131 (between 9 a.m. and 5 p.m. Eastern time). Group discounts are available for study groups, colleges, confirmation classes, and parishes.

# About the Author

S teve Wood has led youth, campus, and pro-life ministries. A graduate of Gordon-Conwell Theological Seminary, he served as an Evangelical pastor for a decade before starting the Family Life Center International in 1992. He is also the founder of St. Joseph's Covenant Keepers, a movement that seeks to transform society through the transformation of fathers and families. Utilizing his book Christian Fatherhood, audio and video tapes, television, radio and conferences, Steve has reached tens of thousands of men in the USA, Canada and overseas with a message of Christian faith and responsibility. He is the host of live Faith and Family broadcasts on EWTN worldwide radio (www.ewtn.com), as well as The Carpenter Shop, an EWTN worldwide television program for fathers.

A member of the American Counseling Association, Steve is also a Certified Family Life Educator. In addition, he is a professional Christian Life Coach with a private practice (www.halftimecoaching.com) offering coaching services for life purpose, lasting relationships, successful marriages, and effective parenting.

Steve and Karen Wood have been married twenty-five years and are the parents of eight children.

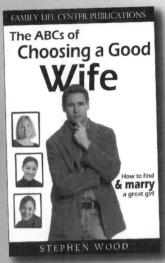